Bungalow Design

Bungalow Design

Chris van Uffelen

BRAUN

Contents

Preface

Bungalows are a place of longing for many people. They are detached dwellings – mostly single-family houses – in which life takes place largely on the first floor. Thus, bungalows often already fulfill important requirements for barrier-free construction. However, the phrase "mostly on the first floor" already shows that there can also be an upper floor, or at least a converted roof. In some places, the generic term "bungalow" has been applied to a specific stylistic form of this type, but the original type and the most common form of bungalow do not have a flat roof. Only in continental Europe did the building type and post-war modernism arrive simultaneously from the United States, so that the term evokes a ground-floor-only flat-roof building in the mind of, for example, a German-speaker. However, the definition of the bungalow does not limit it to the first floor and flat roof at all.

The bungalow, in its present form, originated as a detached, low-rise residential building in India when British colonial officials there adapted the building type for their summer residences. The word also derives from Indian: in Gujarati baṅglo means "Bengali", in Hindi baṅglā means the Bengali house. Houses were small, single-story, and detached with a large porch. Enthralled by their simplicity and functionality, British officials imitated the houses, whose rooms were organized around a central parlor. This concept was adopted as exotic and exclusive in England and later in America. There, the term was used in the late 19th century to describe even very large estate or country houses in completely different stylistic manifestations: with columned porticoes and two full stories plus large gable roofs, possibly including decorative gables, they were much closer to an ancient villa suburbana than to the archetype or a post-war bungalow.

Today, bungalows are one- or one-and-a-half-story detached single-family houses, which usually take up the spatial solutions of apartment floor plans. The upper floor, if any, which extends only partially over the first floor, or the often flat attic, usually contains the washrooms and bedrooms. In most cases, however, these rooms are also on the first floor, which contributes to the living comfort and functionality of this type of building.

The juxtaposition of numerous apartments in a bungalow development is, of course, ecologically questionable, not only in terms of the built-up area, but also in terms of the land occupied by roads and sidewalks in front of and between the individual buildings. The architects are trying to compensate for this with a variety of sustainable strategies, about which this volume also provides information in a separate factual section.

On the other hand, it is precisely the longitudinal extension of the building volume that makes the bungalow aesthetically appealing. One thinks of Ludwig Mies van der Rohe's Barcelona Pavilion at the 1929 World's Fair or post-war buildings such as Philip Johnson's Glass House (New Canaan, 1949). The undivided floor plan, the richness of light from floor-to-ceiling windows, and the simple flat roof panel can be combined in countless configurations. These buildings continue to have an impact in many places and at all times to this day. The chancellor's bungalow in Bonn by Sep Ruf (1964) shows that these buildings were also perceived as highly representative – even if it was not used by most chancellors because it was too modern for them. Whether flat or roofed depends in many places also on the building regulations or the context.

Many of the buildings presented here also use sloping terrain to achieve a flat impression despite the actual larger building volume. But apart from these post-war modernist bungalows, the Indian archetype or American image from the vast suburbia also lives on in modern bungalow construction: The more traditional, single-story longhouse with small windows, gables and chimneys, and wide porch on the street façade lends itself to contemporary reinterpretation. Thus, the history of the building type provides numerous opportunities for reinvention – in individual cases as extensions or even the merging of existing bungalows – that further enrich the image of what a bungalow is.

page 9: Singapore. Bungala for European in federated Malay States
page 11: Ludwig Mies van der Rohe's Barcelona Pavilion, 1929

House on Paros Greece

Architecture: Iwan Bühler Architekten
Completion: 2017
Project address: Oneiron Street, Isterni, Paros, Greece
Bedrooms: 3
Gross floor area: 120 m^2
Size of site: 2,525 m^2

House on Paros

The vacation villa lies in the midst of wildly grown nature with a far-reaching view of the Aegean Sea. The arrow-like structure stretches along the property and welcomes the resident at the tapered top. A narrow path widens into terraces that follow the soft slope of the terrain and eventually reveal views of the Aegean Sea across the pool. Pergolas provide an exciting interplay of light and shadow. Inside, the dining room, kitchen, living room and terraces are arranged one after the other, folding up in width, height and depth, orienting themselves to the view.

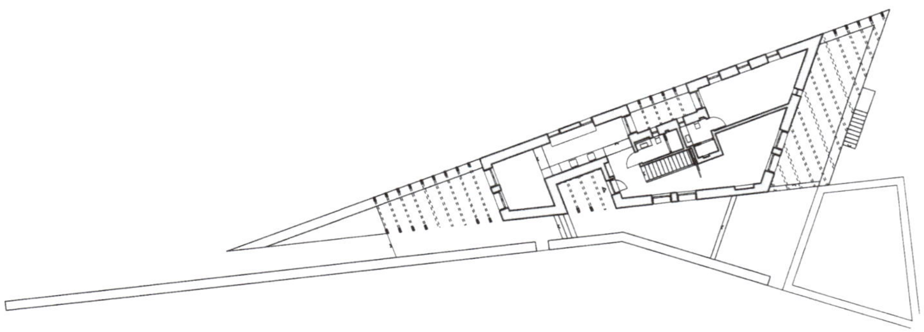

Main materials: masonry; lime plaster; slurry plaster
Ecological aspects: thermal insulation by double-shell masonry thickness 60 cm with interposed air layer; exterior wooden shutters; pergola as sun protection; air-source heat pump as heating since electricity is produced on Paros through a seawater plant

Refuge Brazil

Architecture: Piacesi Arquitetos Associados
Landscape design: Piacesi Arquitetos Associados, Plante comigo
Completion: 2019
Project address: Palácio das Mangabeiras, Belo Horizonte, Brazil
Bedrooms: 1
Gross floor area: 134 m^2

Simplicity and minimalism are the leading concept of the house Refuge, designed for CasaCor Minas, an annual architecture fair. It was inspired by the simplified architecture of Japan and other places around the world. Combined with the idea of digital detoxification, it forms a refuge. The building is projected over metal structures and surrounded by a eucalyptus forest.

It hovers six meters above the ground and the access is formed by a ramp leading through the trees. One façade of the Refuge reflects nature through a mirror element. The interior is connected to the surrounding nature through a glass front. In addition, there is a micro-climatic tension net, which is not only sustainable, but also allows a curved finish without losing transparency.

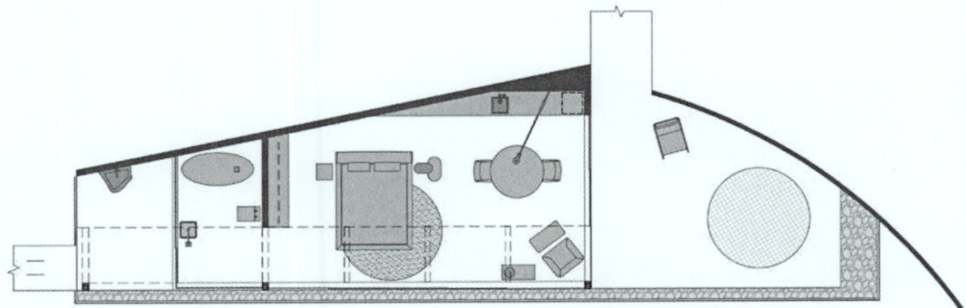

Main materials: glass; steel; concrete; leather; pebbles; cement floor; mirror and revesto textile for façade
Ecological aspects: low cost of execution; metal structure streamlines the process and makes it more sustainable; low volume of debris

Villa AT Norway

Architecture: Saunders Architecture
Interior design: Hannes Wingate
Completion: 2016
Project address: Søgne, Kristiansand, Norway
Bedrooms: 3
Gross floor area: 310 m^2
Size of site: 4,000 m^2

Villa AT is located on a generous site with a high vantage point. The L-shaped main house is set alongside a stand-alone guest house by the drive. The entrance hall is positioned at the center of this pivot. To the left runs a glazed corridor leading to two bedrooms, a top-lit family bathroom, and the master bedroom. To the right, the open plan kitchen and dining room are located, separated from the living room by a central concrete hearth. The fireplace creates a warm focal point, while still allowing for easy family communication between the two areas. The house sits on a podium, with wraparound terraces and steps made of local stone leading down to a swimming pool. Slatted timber ceilings mirror the exterior façade, which in turn evokes the areas traditionally built houses. At the same time, it contrasts these boxy, conventional forms with a curving façade that uses wood in a fluid, contemporary way.

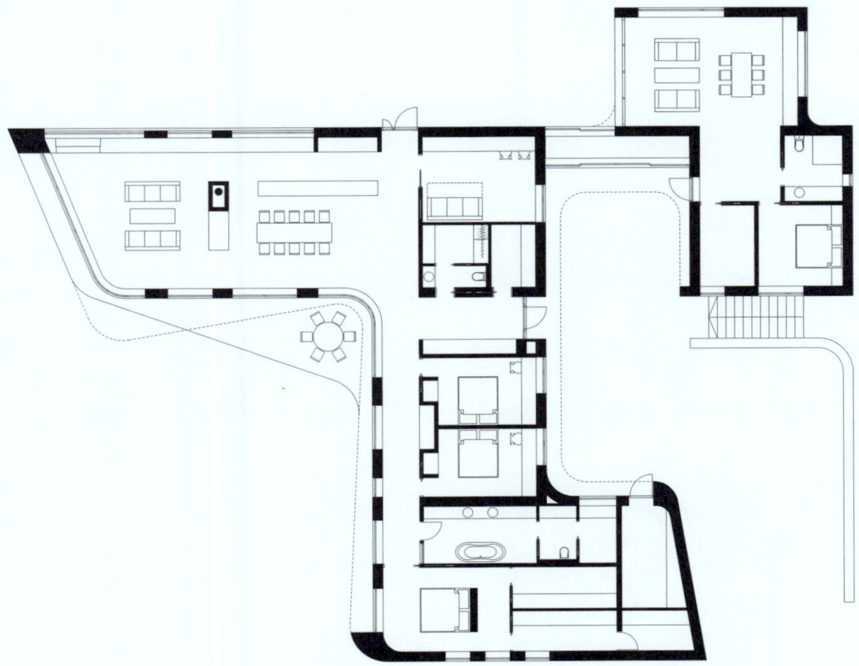

Main materials: wood; spruce; thermo ash; Norwegian stone Hardanger/Jondal; planed and oiled oak planks; acrylic stone; Ariostea tiles
Ecological aspects: two geothermal heat pumps; water in floor heating; triple-glazed windows; 300 mm insulation in walls

Klobbudden Sweden

Architecture: John Robert Nilsson Arkitektkontor
Completion: 2018
Project address: Stockholm, Sweden
Bedrooms: 4
Gross floor area: 525 m^2
Size of site: 13,000 m^2

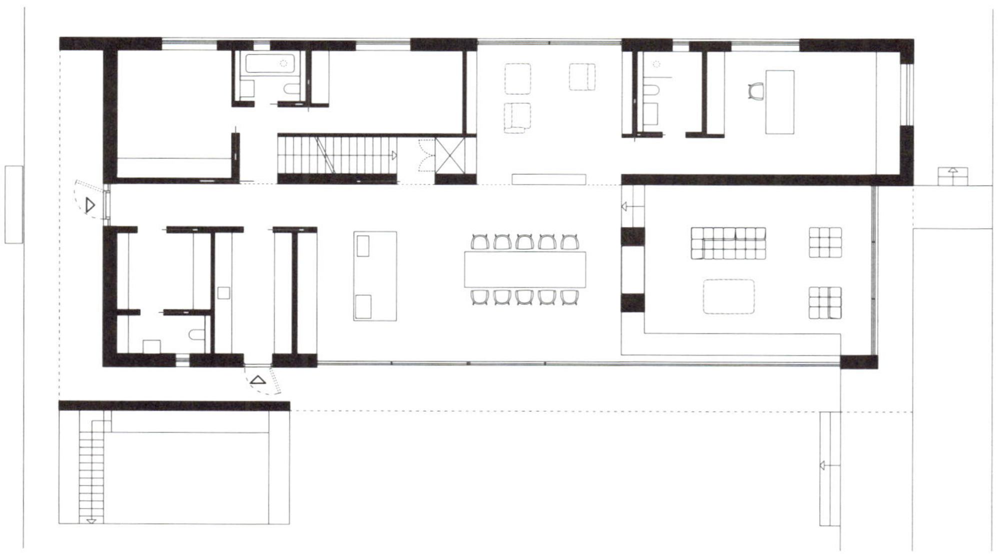

The former radio station from the 1950s is situated on top of a vast granite rock on a peninsula in Stockholm. The unique building site offers both, magnificent views and privacy, provided by a small pine tree forest. The limestone base forms a clear separation from the natural ground. Inside the house, high ceilings and generous glass openings provide both, light and panoramic views for the social areas, seamlessly connecting indoors and outdoors. A lower ceiling height in the private rooms creates a protected private rooftop space with fantastic views.

Main materials: limestone; glass; cedar; walnut
Ecological aspects: thermal heat

Mid-Century Bungalow Germany

Architecture: Corneille Uedingslohmann Architekten
Completion: 2016
Project address: Cologne, Germany
Bedrooms: 3
Gross floor area: 325 m^2
Size of site: 2,023 m^2
Original completion: 1959

The Mid-Century Bungalow was carefully restored and modernized in 2016. The existing L-shaped building is structured over three layered ceiling slices and was extended on both sides. The living and sleeping areas are located under the two lower slices, while the central zone with entrance, kitchen and dining area is located under the higher one. The sleeping wing was extended at ground level and three barrel roofs were added to extend the ceiling height in the newly created space. On the street-facing side, the house appears closed off, while it opens up to the wide garden. Into the garden, the building was extended on the upper floor by a cube, which can be opened completely on the garden side by folding shutters. The then exposed interior contains a fitness and wellness area with sauna. The first floor area under the cube was completely glazed on all sides. With the floor covering running from the outside to the inside, the character of an outdoor studio is created.

Main materials: concrete; glass; steel; cedarwood cladding
Ecological aspects: improved insulation; hot water partly heated by photovoltaic

Cork Trees House Portugal

Architecture: TRAMA Arquitetos
Interior design: TRAMA Arquitetos + OLIVEGREY – Atelier e Showroom de Design de Interiores
Completion: 2020
Project address: Braga, Portugal
Bedrooms: 4
Gross floor area: 560 m^2
Size of site: 2,471m^2

The specifications for the project included a harmonious design and a focus on the space details. The intention was to surprise, to integrate the exterior surroundings with the interior environment, to merge spaces and create sensations, without discouraging functionality. The name of the Cork Trees House reflects the fundamental role that the native vegetation plays in its architecture. The terrain, on a steep slope, is composed of a grove of century-old cork oak trees, located on the lowest level. In this context, the house was designed to enjoy the best sun exposure and also the open views over the mountains and valleys of the region. In order to place the floor of the house at the same height as the canopy of cork oaks, a functional one-story floor plan was designed, which occupies almost the entire width of the plot. This creates the effect of a floating garden on the horizon. On the inside, the raw and natural materials provide comfort, harmony and a timeless design.

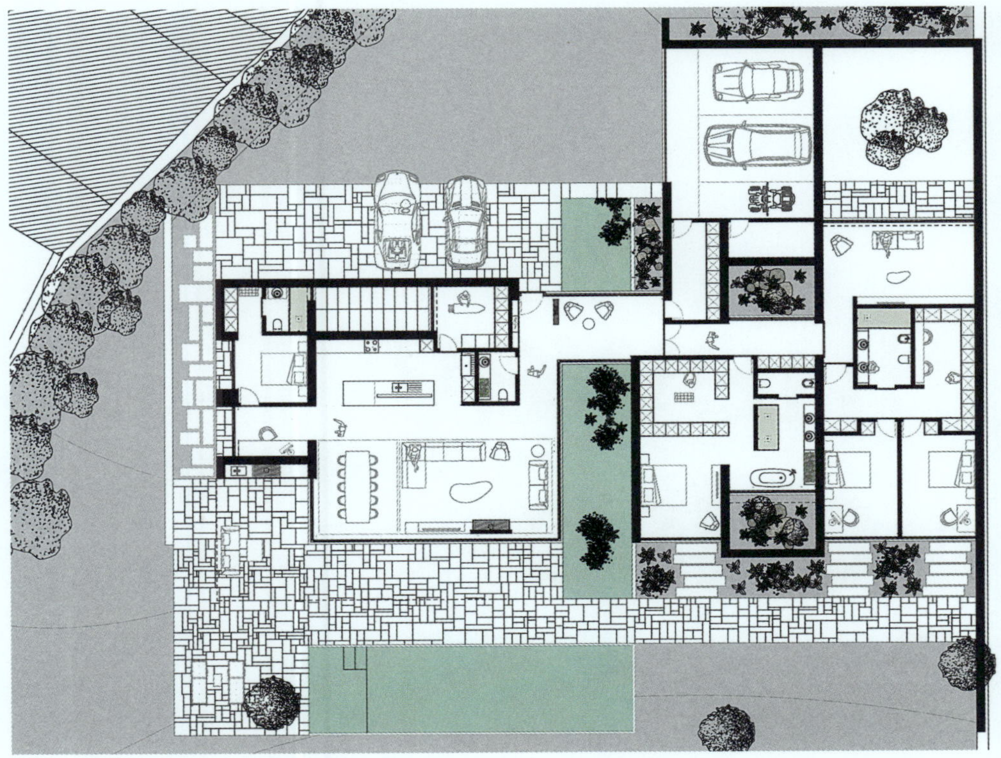

Main materials: black slate; pre-weathered steel; concrete; walnut wood; Roman travertine
Ecological aspects: home automation system; photovoltaic solar panels

Fineway House Germany

Architecture: Alexander Brenner Architekten
Completion: 2020
Project address: Reutlingen, Germany
Bedrooms: 3
Gross floor area: 500 m^2
Size of site: 1,850 m^2

This modern, spacious villa was built on a site near Reutlingen near a popular hiking path. To the north, facing this path, it appears stony, solid and closed. It opens up with floor-to-ceiling glazing to the view side in the south. Here, the view wanders across the pool to the wide valley. For energy reasons and sustainability, the exterior walls are made of 50-centimeter-thick aerated concrete and a 25-centimeter-thick processed exposed concrete shell. With the addition of local Jurassic grit, it appears a warm grayish beige after machining. The façade, worked by hand through pointing, stocking and scarfing, presents itself with a rough relief structure. Inside, stonemasons also created a very special atmosphere by using bush-hammered concrete on fixtures, stairs and balustrades, reminiscent of the stone strength of historic buildings. The soothing feeling of solidity and durability is reinforced by whitewashed walls, natural stone flooring and oak parquet.

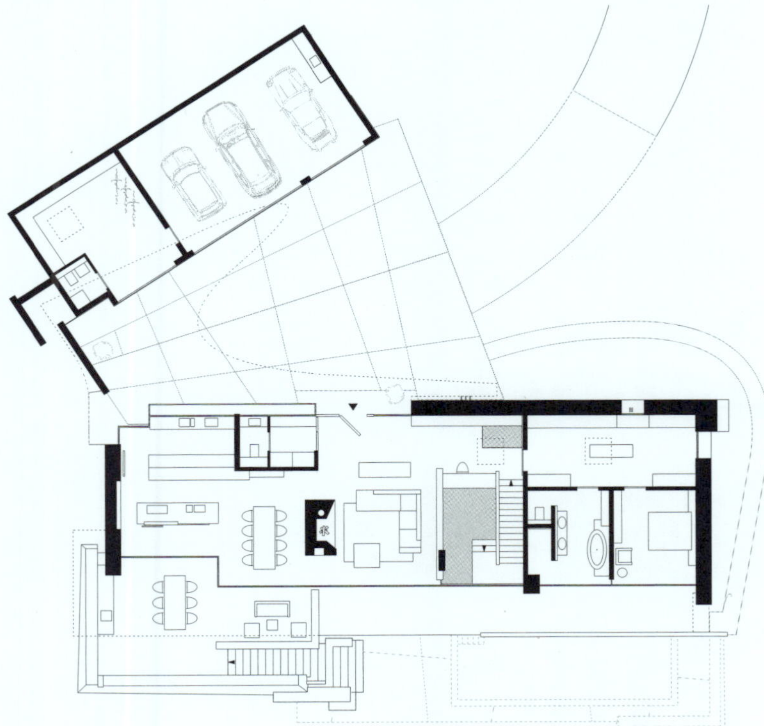

Main materials: concrete; mineral plaster; lime plaster; shell limestone; oak in various finishes; linoleum
Ecological aspects: exterior walls made of 50-centimeter-thick aerated concrete and a machined exposed concrete shell of 25 centimeters

Casa Prefab Chile

Architecture: DX Arquitectos
Completion: 2017
Project address: Camino El Volcan 10702,
9460000 San José de Maipo, Chile
Bedrooms: 2
Gross floor area: 90 m^2
Size of site: 5,000 m^2

This project is designed to meet the needs of a couple who wanted to build a house in the city of San José de Maipo, Chile. Among the main requirements were a flexible room layout that would enhance the view of the property and a prefabricated construction system that would minimize the amount of work required on site. In response, the program was developed in an elongated volume with a completely transparent façade in an east-west direction. The main central space is a living-dining room with integrated kitchen.

At the two ends of the house, two bedrooms, two bathrooms and a loggia are distributed. The construction method was based on the production of three modules, which were manufactured in a factory in Santiago and then transported to the site to be assembled into the final volume.

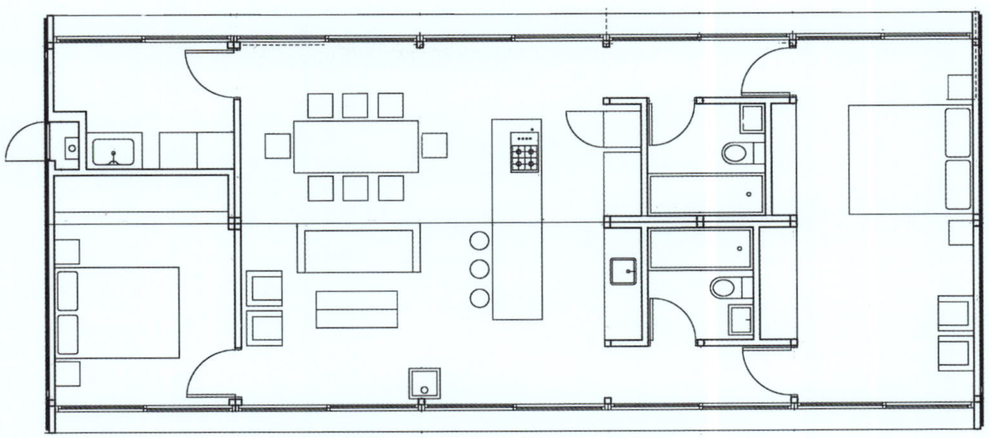

Main materials: steel; wood
Ecological aspects: excellent thermal insulation based on expanded polystyrene

Laurel Hills Residence USA

Architecture: Assembledge+
Interior design: Susan Mitnick Design Studio
Landscape design: Fiore Landscape Design
Completion: 2019
Project address: Los Angeles, CA, USA
Bedrooms: 5
Gross floor area: 455 m^2
Size of site: 1,675 m^2

The single-story residence is composed of three pavilions. The living pavilion in the west, the sleeping pavilion in the east, and the guest house/garage pavilion are connected by a series of glass hallways. A walkway of concrete pavers, lined by wild grasses, leads to the front door, passing a tranquil courtyard with olive trees. The entry to the house is located within a glass hallway, connecting the sleeping and the living pavilion. Large windows, skylights, and pocketing doors infuse the home with natural light, reflecting off wooden floors and marble countertops. The fluidity between the kitchen, breakfast room and family room, designed for uninterrupted entertainment, creates a harmony of transparency and lightness. Outside, the 12-meter pool and ample space create a series of outdoor rooms. The surrounding trees and hills are taken to be the building envelope and the exterior walls of the house are reconceived as a series of partition walls.

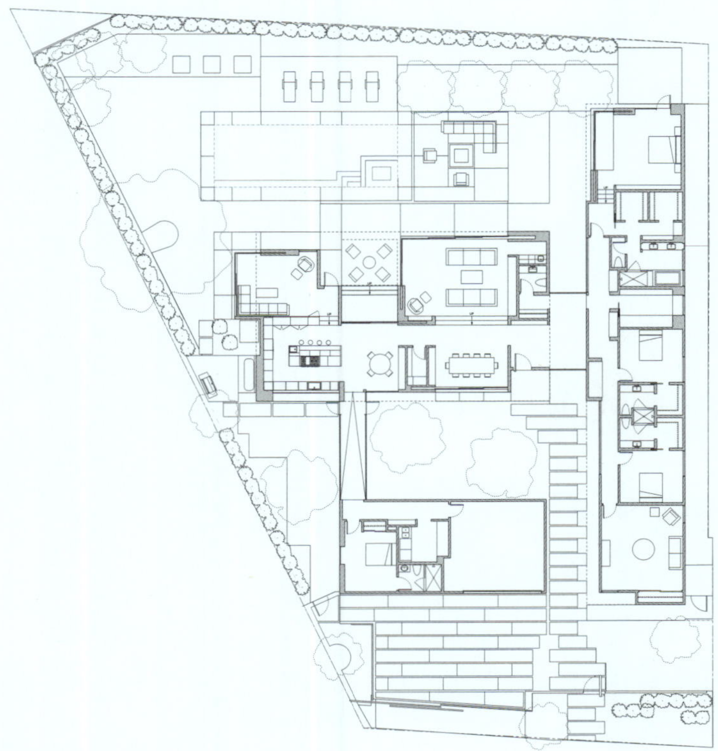

Main materials: western red cedar; painted cement board; glass
Ecological aspects: low massing to utilize shading from surrounding trees with large roof for solar; overhangs to south; reflective roof surfaces; LED lighting; high efficiency HVAC systems; rainwater collection; drought-tolerant landscaping

Planar House Brazil

Architecture: Studio MK27
Interior design: Diana Radomysler
Landscape design: Maria João d'Orey
Completion: 2018
Project address: Porto Feliz, São Paulo, Brazil
Bedrooms: 5
Gross floor area: 1,000 m²
Size of site: 7,000 m²

Planar House is a radical exercise in horizontality designed by architects Marcio Kogan and Lair Reis. Inside, the space is divided in two areas. The first one with the service areas, gym, tv- and playrooms, and the second one with the five en-suite bedrooms. The living rooms are located at the extreme ends and can be completely opened by sliding glass doors, transforming the entire house into a terrace. The interiors are made of low and solid wood furniture. A translucent multi-colored club chair hanging from the slab becomes the focus of attention and contrasts with the horizontality of the house.

The building is discreetly positioned at the highest point of the plot, favoring the existing topography. This particular location demanded care and attention with the design of the rooftop, which is the fifth façade of the building. The equipment placed on the roof, such as solar panels and skylights, was carefully composed and selected. The green roof mimics the surrounding lawn and contributes to the thermal comfort inside. Surrounding the rigid formal distribution, there is a vertical winding wall made of solid bricks arranged in solids and voids.

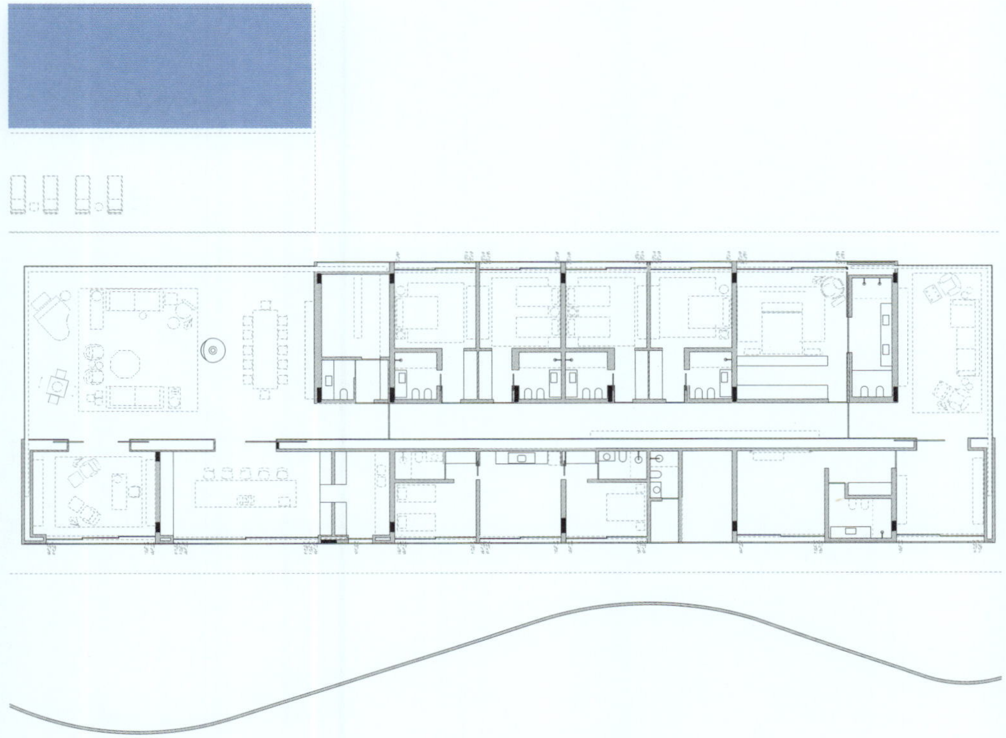

Main materials: stone; wood panels; aluminum; steel; glass
Ecological aspects: green roof for thermal comfort in the house; solar panels

Examilia House Greece

Architecture: Katerina Valsamaki Architects
Completion: 2017
Project address: Examilia, Korinthos, Peloponnese, Greece
Bedrooms: 3
Gross floor area: 137 m^2
Size of site: 4,200 m^2

The white single-story vacation house is located on an altitude of 80 meters from the sea. A path running parallel to the house leads to the entrance. A row of trees inside the unroofed courtyard, which complements the exterior of the house on this side, emphasizes the idea of the cloister. Upon entering the house, the spatial continuity between the interior and exterior living areas becomes apparent. The open living areas have floor-to-ceiling sliding windows that capture natural light on all three sides while providing views of the garden, the city and the sea.

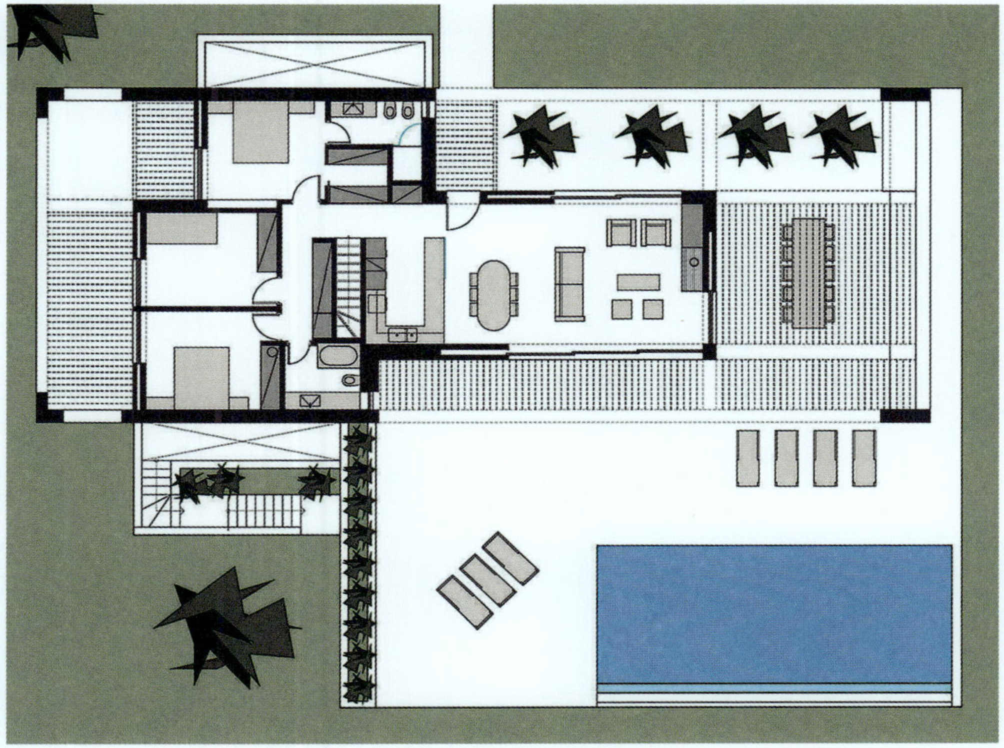

Main materials: plastered reinforced concrete; bricks; tiles
Ecological aspects: solar heating; water collection; bio tank; recycling of the organic waste

Hill Country House USA

Architecture: Miró Rivera Architects
Completion: 2017
Project address: Wimberley, TX, USA
Bedrooms: 3
Gross floor area: 475 m^2
Size of site: 190,000 m^2

Conceived as a prototype for a sustainable rural community, the Hill Country House serves as an example to show what could be: A self-sustaining home in a rural setting, virtually independent of municipal water and energy. Situated on a sweeping Texas Hill Country meadow, this private residence is defined by a series of jagged roof peaks inspired by the rise and fall of the surrounding hills. Lovingly referred to as "The Sanctuary" by its owners, an active retired couple, this modern take on the farm house style is a place to bring people together and find spiritual renewal in a responsible, sustainable setting. The exterior of the home is defined by clean lines and a sculptural gable roof. Stark white corrugated metal panel is broken at various intervals by warm cypress siding that defines a series of rooms outside the house, including a temple-like screen porch and an outdoor sculpture studio that doubles as a stage at gatherings 3–4 times a year.

In plan, a collection of volumes is arranged along a central spine reminiscent of vernacular "shotgun" cabins, with the public and private spaces of the home situated on opposite ends. In every room, windows provide abundant natural light and frame views of the surrounding landscape. Throughout the interior, white walls and ceilings are offset by touches of limestone and soapstone, while pecan floors nod to the home's rustic locale. The design is both spiritually and environmentally sensitive, earning a 4-star rating from the nation's first green building program.

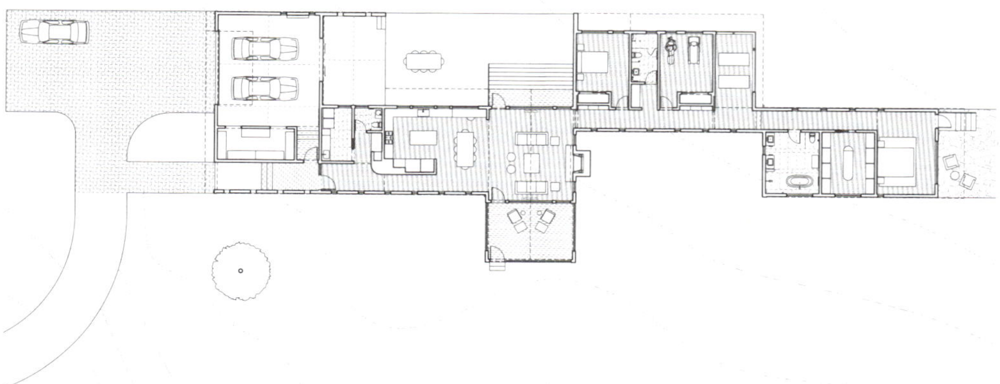

Main materials: cypress wood; pecan wood; dry-stacked local limestone; corrugated metal; aluminum; glass
Ecological aspects: solar energy; geothermal heating/cooling; rainwater collection; local materials; low embodied energy; construction waste management and recycling; zero-VOC paints and coatings

Villa Marie Austria

Architecture: Superfuturegroup
Completion: 2019
Project address: Am Römerweg 2, 4550 Kremsmünster, Austria
Bedrooms: 3
Gross floor area: 295 m^2
Size of site: 1,129 m^2

Villa Marie is situated on a south-orientated slope in the alpine foothill region of Upper Austria, which is characterized by soft hills and splendid views to the alps. The design focuses on two aspects, a bungalow concept organizes all rooms on one level around a central living area and the west orientated veranda terrace. The generous veranda connects the main living room with the garden and provides a covered, outdoor social area. The living area is divided into the kitchen area, the fireplace and seating area, and cabinets and storage space. The wooden bungalow touches the ground on the north and opens up an entrance and service level in the basement. Light wood, as main material of floor and ceiling, defines the atmosphere in the house and is contrasted with dark colored wood and fiber cement boards for the façade. The interiors are open and light. All the materials, textures, colors and the open layout enable the bungalow to become a versatile yet highly efficient living space.

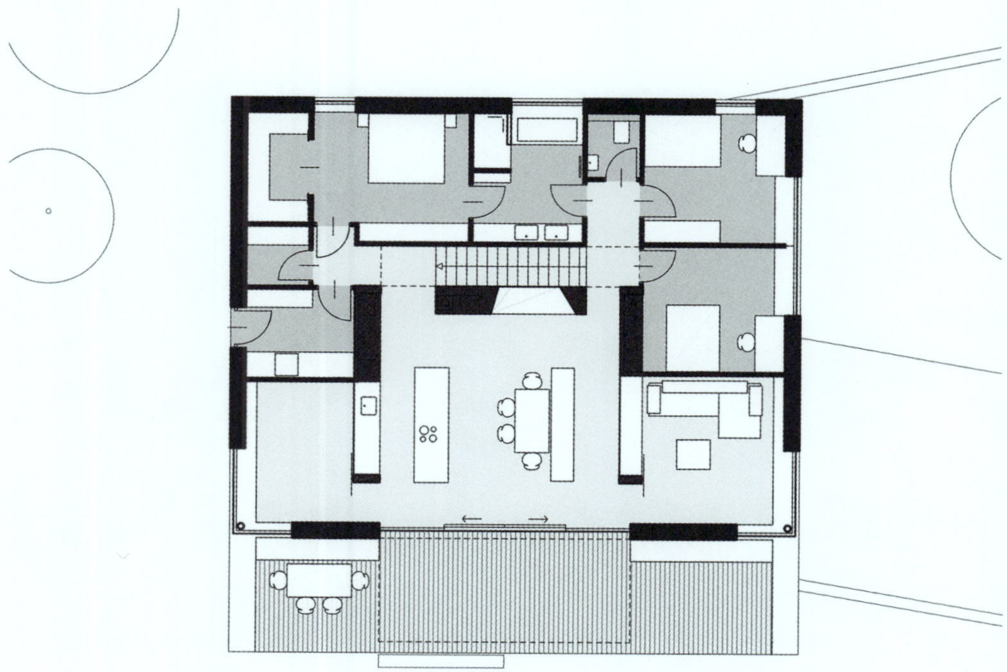

Main materials: solid wood construction; wooden façade
Ecological aspects: wood construction; heat pump; living space ventilation

Folding Roof House For Two Austria

Architecture: Abendroth Architekten
Completion: 2020
Project address: Langenzersdorf, Austria
Bedrooms: 2
Gross floor area: 150 m^2
Size of site: 820 m^2

The building is covered by a folded roof, which can be experienced from the inside. The wooden structure is always visible, even though the façade has been covered with plaster. The entrance also works as a workplace and consists of a flexible open area connected to the new living space. A loggia in front of the living room provides shade with its slat-like border. The terrain is gently raised and ends level at the wooden deck, that surrounds the living space from the outside. Accessibility is consistently realized in this bungalow.

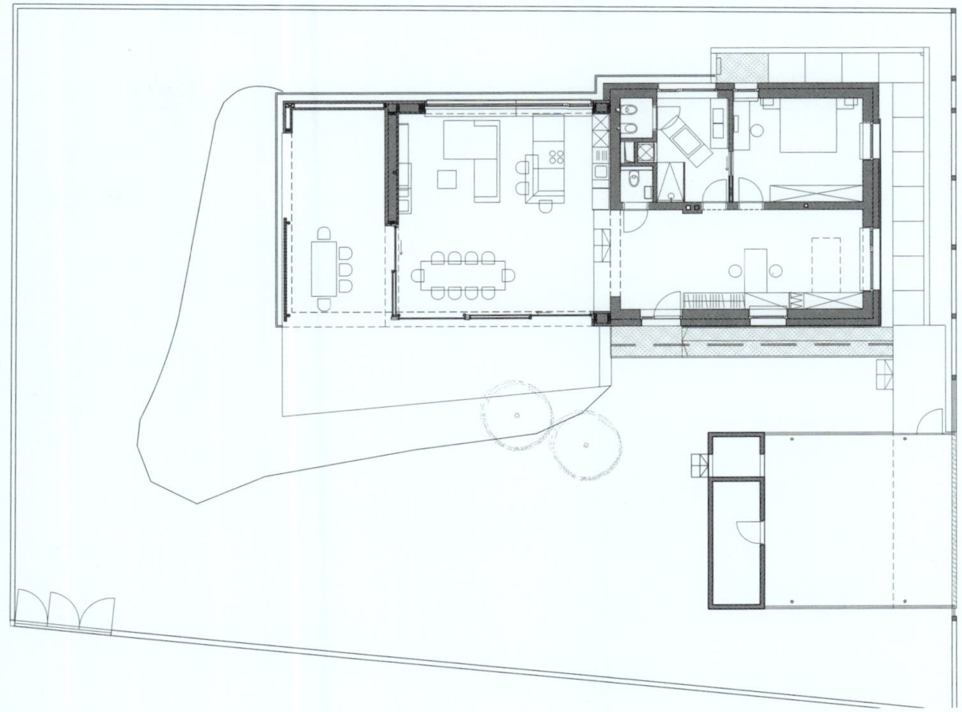

Main materials: wood; glass; metal; plastered surfaces
Ecological aspects: redensification in wood frame construction; geothermal heat pump

House V+M Germany

Architecture: Platter Architekten
Completion: 2018
Project address: Salzgitter, Germany
Bedrooms: 2
Gross floor area: 223 m^2
Size of site: 639 m^2

The first external impression of the bungalow is characterized by the two opposing, gray monopitch roofs, which are separated by a flat roof section. Under one pent roof is the living area, under the other pent roof is the sleeping area. Located in between are the entrance, hallway, kitchen and dining area. The floor plan of the house V+M has an H-shape, which is filled to the south with a patio between the living and sleeping areas. Strictly speaking, a patio refers in Spanish and Portuguese to a courtyard in the center of a townhouse. The V+M house is actually not a townhouse, but is located in a new building area. However, the patio with the kitchen forms the center of the house. Centrally located and protected from prying eyes, the patio creates a secluded place for eating, grilling, celebrating, sunbathing, lounging and dreaming between the white plastered walls. For visitors, the patio forms the surprise of the house.

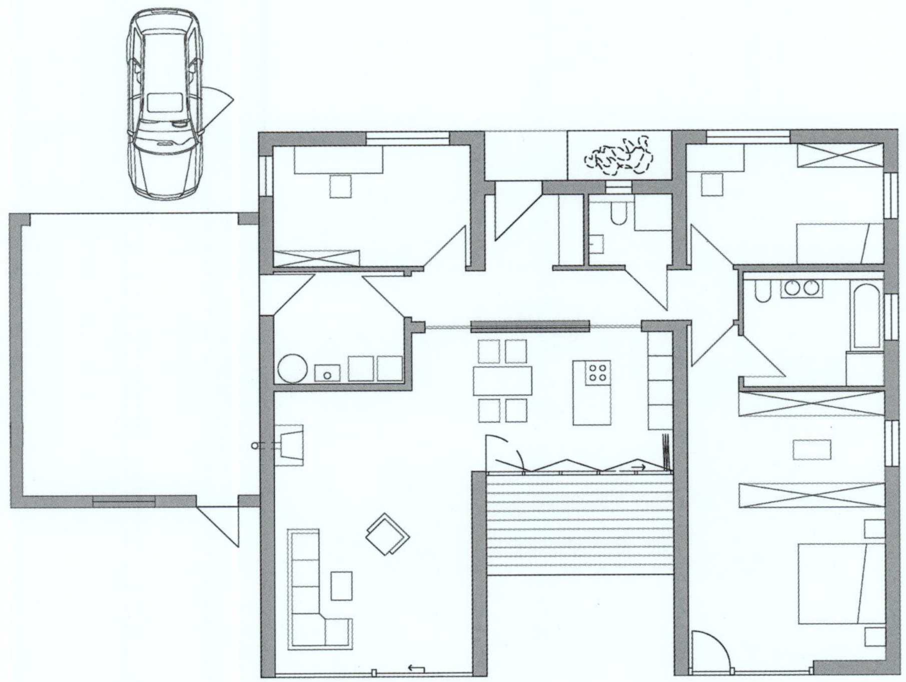

Main materials: brick; wood; zinc sheet
Ecological aspects: heating and domestic hot water heating via natural gas and solar thermal; decentralized ventilation system with heat recovery; energy standard KfW efficiency house 70 (based on EnEV 2014)

Two Sheds Australia

Architecture: DREAMER with Roger Nelson
Landscape design: Eckerley Garden Architecture / Scott Leung
Completion: 2019
Project address: 90 Grove Road, Lorne, Victoria, Australia
Bedrooms: 3
Gross floor area: 220 m^2
Size of site: 101,000 m^2
Client: Roger and Jane Nelson

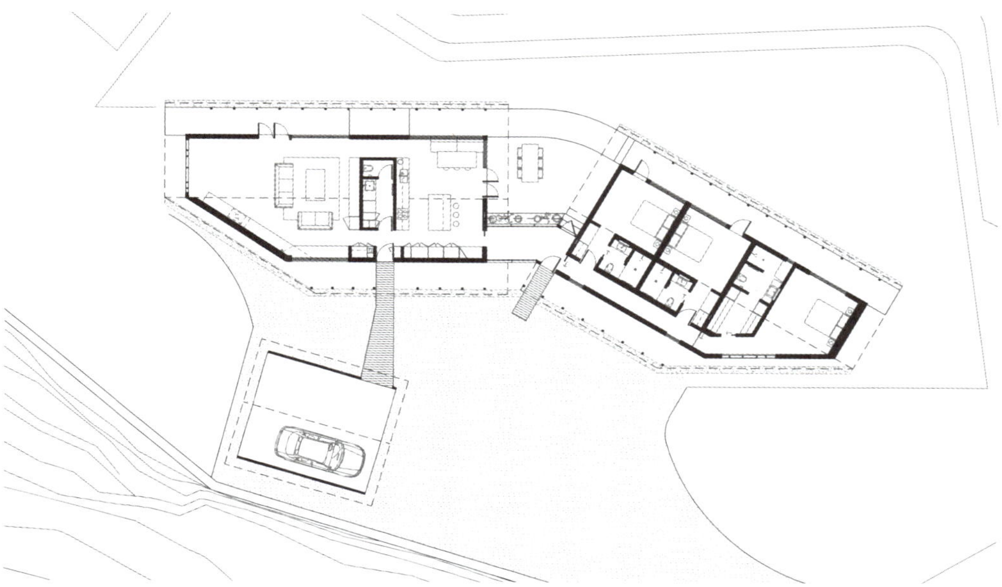

Two Sheds is a house of elegant simplicity and imperfect loveliness. The reductive approach taken during design process minimized the number of materials and highlighted the pared back, familiar design. The focus of the project was more on the creation of beautiful space rather than on a perfect example of architecture. The result is a house that is calm, flexible, and with opportunities for family connection and ease of working in the landscape and nearby bush. The simple roof, veranda and cladding allow the building to sit easily in the landscape within the magical backdrop of the surrounding bush and hills. There is a timeless feeling to the house, and we look forward to watching how the brass and timber develop their own personalities as they age over time. Two Sheds is a project that helps to define what a regionally appropriate Australian architecture can look like. Its gable roof form and veranda leads back to classic Australian cottages, sheds and cabins.

These icons of rural built form and associated design elements are important to Australian culture. A design methodology that looks to the past in the creation of Australian rural housing may hold the key to ensure that successful buildings that connect to landscape are climate appropriate and flexible to future change.

Main materials: timber frame; timber cladding internally and externally; galvanized steel roof
Ecological aspects: local and sustainably sourced materials; walls and roof high performing thermally; no air conditioning; brass instead of chromed fittings for sanitary; low volatile organic compound materials used; LED lights

Holly Water Cabin England

Architecture: Out of the Valley
Completion: 2020
Project address: Marsh Farm, Cheriton Fitzpaine, Devon, England
Bedrooms: 1
Gross floor area: 70 m^2
Size of site: 18,211 m^2
Client: Ed and Sara Burnand

Holly Water is a resort in the heart of Devon, United Kingdom. It offers its residents a close relationship with nature and at the same time the highest level of comfort. A path that winds through a cornfield leads to the cedar-clad house. Its exterior is characterized by a large shed roof with generous eaves. Inside, an oak kitchen occupies the back wall of the open interior, while a bathroom and a cozy sleeping area with a double bed are integrated into the gable end. Sliding doors open from the living space onto a curved larch veranda with a copper tub for soaking in nature.

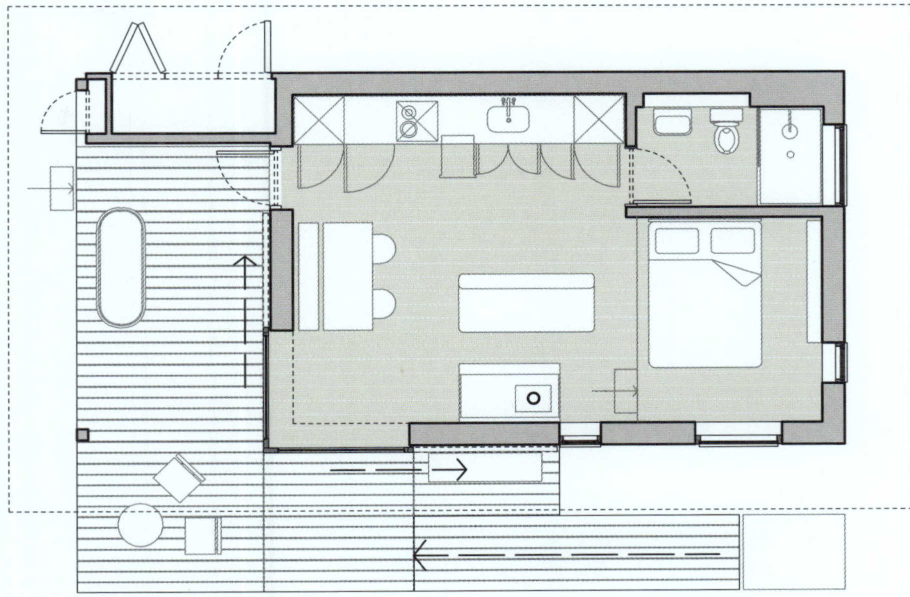

Main materials: Douglas fir; oak; larch; cedar; clay plaster; jute
Ecological aspects: local timbers; plant-based insulations; clay internal render

Goodtown Australia

Architecture: Alexandra Buchanan Architecture
Landscape design: Lush Landscape Solutions
Completion: 2019
Project address: Rochedale, Australia
Bedrooms: 4
Gross floor area: 610 m^2
Size of site: 1,900 m^2

Goodtown House is a beautifully crafted, texturally rich contemporary courtyard home. The expansive, one-story house sits gently on the site, where subtle elevations control the landscape and orientation. The building features large eaves to the north, which provide necessary shading for the skylights below. Skylights above the doors promote natural air circulation and the infiltration of soft light into the living areas. An interplay of levels, interconnected interior living spaces, and the relationship to the outdoors creates a multi-faceted, yet private living experience.

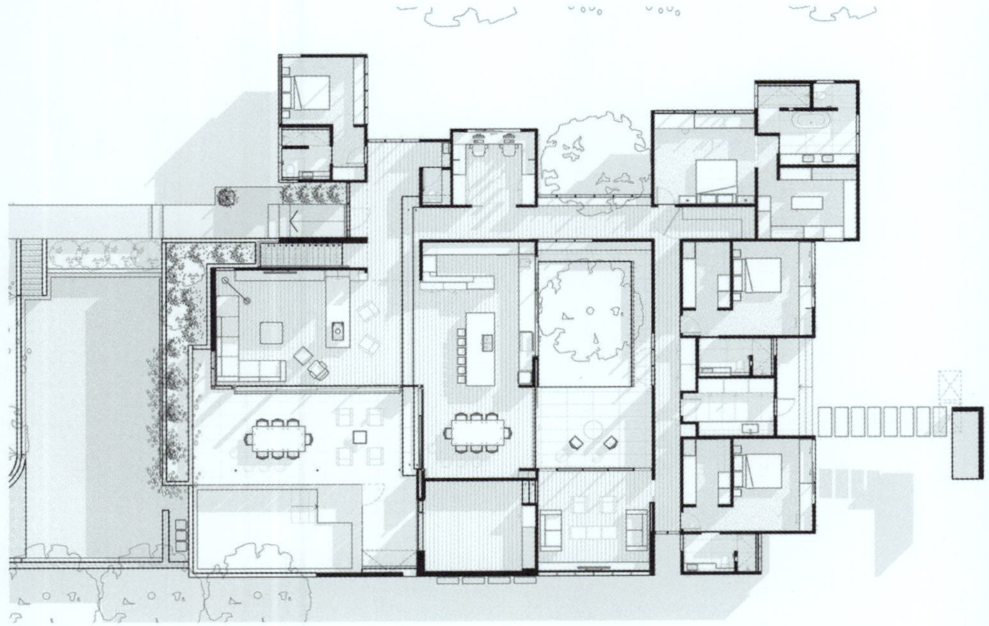

Main materials: timber; concrete; steel; glass
Ecological aspects: timber cladding with no chemical additives; significant overhangs to alleviate thermal heat gain in summer; central courtyard creates cross ventilation; central courtyard spills natural light into the center of the house

Camelia
USA

Architecture: Baran Studio Architecture
Completion: 2019
Project address: Camelia Lane, Walnut Creek, CA, USA
Bedrooms: 3
Gross floor area: 242.3 m^2
Size of site: 2,152 m^2
Client: Jen Brann and Josh Brann

Camelia is a comprehensive renovation and re-imagining of an existing 1950s ranch house into a modern, open light-filled, bungalow-style home. The finished house does not resemble the former home's period fixtures and small enclosed rooms.

Inspiration was taken from the existing structure to inform the architectural interventions. The entry, located between the garage and bedroom wing, is highlighted by large sidelight windows and a linear foyer skylight. The overhangs are extended to provide further shade and weather protection, while new single pitch roof lines allow clerestories and new high ceilings. The rear yard is accessed by a large center part sliding door, fully connecting interior and exterior spaces. The open kitchen offers a seamless flow between spaces, a light wood clad set of stairs leads up to the new office loft, and the guest bathroom includes a surprising infinity skylight, which adds a fascinating element to a typically mundane space.

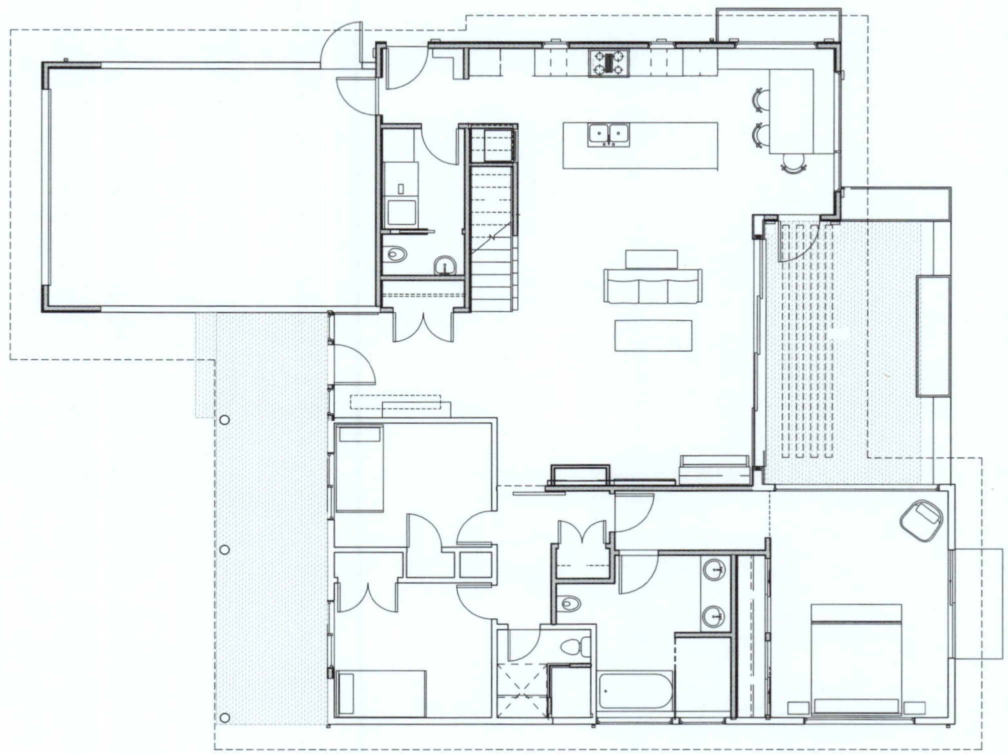

Main materials: pinewood; redwood; sheetrock; paint
Ecological aspects: meets California Green requirements with energy use; reuse and recycling of materials; indoor environmental quality

Sugar Shack Residence USA

Architecture: alterstudio architecture
Completion: 2016
Project address: West Lake Hills, TX, USA
Bedrooms: 4
Gross floor area: 331 m^2
Size of site: 1,922 m^2

The Sugar Shack Residence is embedded between a steep ravine and a more sedate outdoor pool and garden. The house bends to accommodate its surrounding landscape which determines the organization of the interior spaces. Located at the inflection of the bend is a breakfast nook, which is articulated by a niche clad in blue velvet, a small pendant and an Eero Saarinen table.

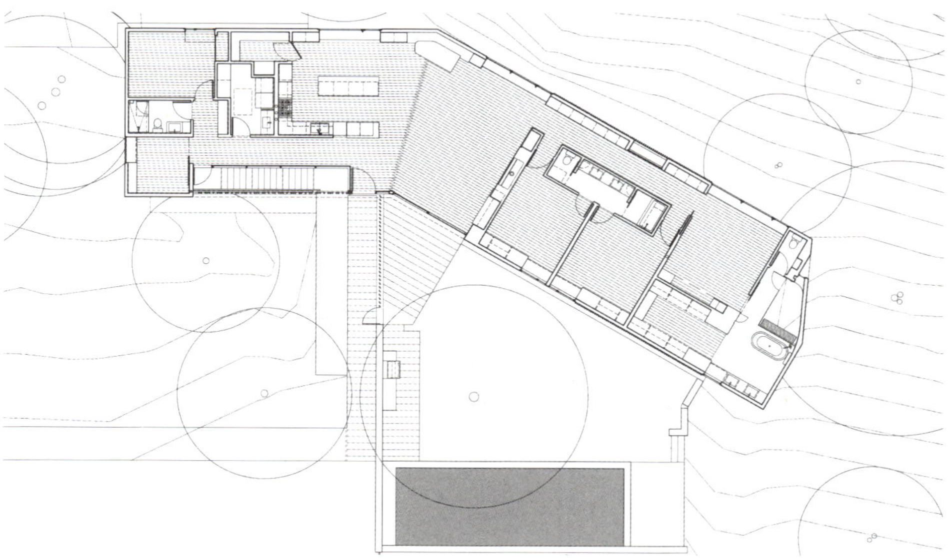

Adjacent to this is the living area which opens up and brings natural light deep into the house. The windows in the house were laid out to block neighboring views while maximizing natural light. Throughout the house, the ceiling is as free of elements as possible, forming a continuous plane. The ceiling fixtures are grouped in a steel housing as well as electrical outlets, light and media controls were recessed into steel panels to minimize their visual impact. In combination with the light and dark materials, the focus is not only on the interior but also on the surrounding landscape.

Main materials: clear sealed steel; white oak; raw concrete
Ecological aspects: shade by trees; natural materials and traditional methods used; minimized use of chemicals

Bungalow Germering Germany

Architecture: Arnold / Werner and Kurt Tillich
Completion: 2016
Project address: Germering, Germany
Bedrooms: 4
Gross floor area: 250 m^2
Size of site: 1,000 m^2

The L-shaped bungalow from the sixties was demolished to the foundation walls, gutted and rebuilt on the old floor plan. The new house is equipped with a hipped roof, which is common in this residential area, and provides space for two children's rooms, a gallery open to the living room on the ground floor, an office and a bathroom. On the first floor, a spacious entrance area with a checkroom, guest toilet, a comfortable bench, and access to the upper floor are located.

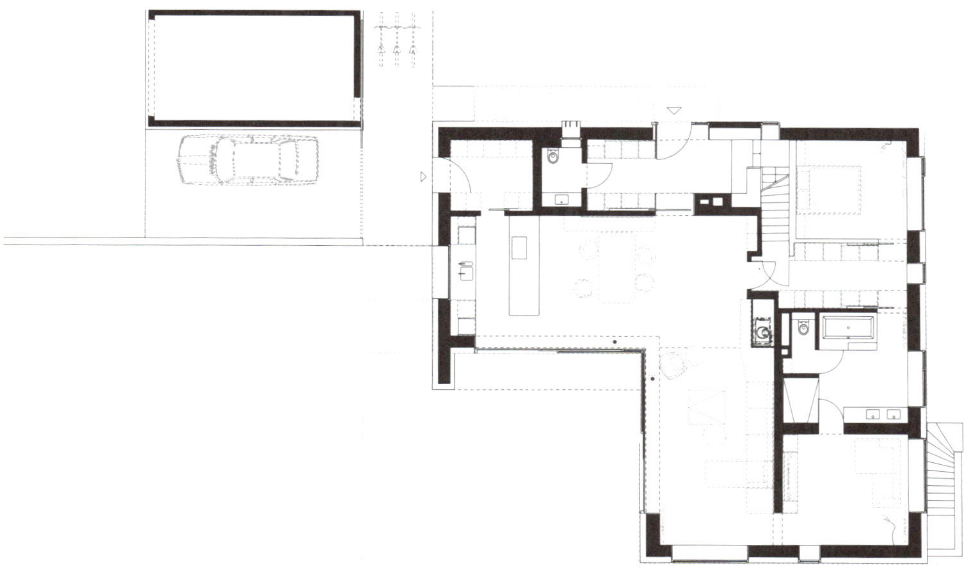

From the entrance, the view opens into the living and dining areas of the house and onto the terrace. Due to large sliding glass elements, threshold-free transition and a column-free interior corner, a space continuum is created between inside and outside. Along the east side façade, master bedroom, dressing room and master bath seamlessly line up, separable by sliding doors.

Main materials: exposed screed; oak wood; shell limestone from Kirchheim
Ecological aspects: solar system on the carport

Bredeney House Germany

Architecture: Alexander Brenner Architekten
Completion: 2015
Project address: Essen, Germany
Bedrooms: 5
Gross floor area: 725 m^2
Size of site: 2,375 m^2

The Bredeney House is oriented in its restraint towards the early buildings of its quarter. It intends to appear like a quiet and timeless urban building block, that had always been there. The interior lies naturally on the found topography. The four-meter-high first floor with kitchen, dining and living room is connected by a hall to the wing, where the private rooms are located. Half a floor higher, the parents' area is located, while the realm for children and guests is staggered half a floor down. The garden is crossed by the elongated terrace, which ends in a cubic pavilion.

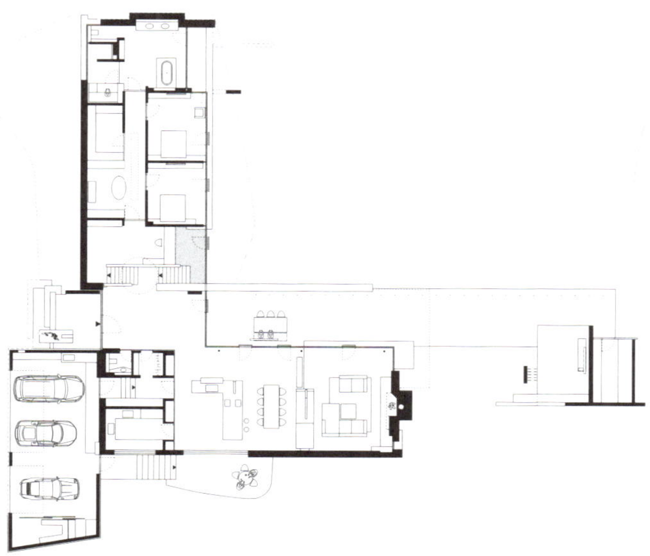

Main materials: concrete; mineral plaster; lime plaster; basalt; oak wood; lacquer; copper and bronze coating
Ecological aspects: to avoid composite thermal insulation system, external aerated concrete walls in thicknesses between 50 and 65 cm; mineral paints inside and outside of the house

Project Ö
Finland

Architecture: Aleksi Hautamäki
Completion: 2019
Project address: Archipelago National Park, Finland
Bedrooms: 1
Gross floor area: 70 m^2
Size of site: 20,234 m^2

The summer cabin with a sauna and the workshop pay tribute to the traditional Finnish archipelago aesthetics with cabled roof, long eaves, extended gutters and vertical cladding. The vision was to have all things necessary with as little space as possible. The project uses solar power for energy and filtered sea water for drinking.

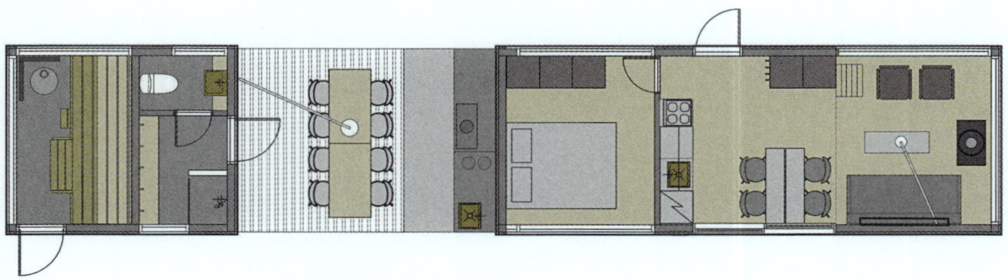

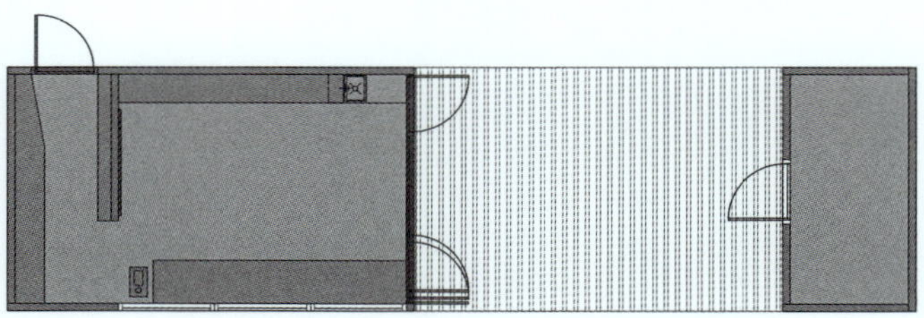

Main materials: pine log
Ecological aspects: self-sufficient in electricity, water and heating

accurate and timeless Switzerland

Architecture: Gisler Architektur und Bauplanung
Completion: 2019
Project address: Unterbächli 170b,
3857 Unterbach near Meiringen, Switzerland
Bedrooms: 2
Gross floor area: 129 m^2
Size of site: 1,540 m^2

The wooden bungalow stands in a small valley village. The building should provide barrier-free living, integrate itself confidentially into the rural environment, and may stand out from the surrounding buildings. Built on a massive base, the house refers in form and materialization to the local building tradition. Through the monopitch roof form, the building volume stands out more as a small or secondary building, to avoid competing with the three-story main house and the surrounding higher residential buildings.

Clear lines and distinct change of materials intend to stimulate discussion and create thoughts. The rectangular floor plan grid distributes the respective uses based on the cardinal directions as well as the local weather conditions. These also lead to the different façade surfaces and the choice of canopy locations.

Main materials: wood; concrete
Ecological aspects: local wood; alignment; settlement

House in Huentelauquen Chile

Architecture: Pablo Saric Arquitectos + Winckler Arquitectos
Completion: 2020
Project address: Huentelauquen Norte, Chile
Bedrooms: 3
Gross floor area: 125.5 m²
Size of site: 5,000 m²
Client: Barbara Sole and Pablo Saric

House in Huentelauquen is located 85 meters from the coastline, with native vegetation, constant sun throughout the year and frequent wind. The house opens to the view of the sea and inside, the rooms are located at the ends, freeing the glazed center for the common use areas. The walls arranged in the east-west direction create wind shadows.

Main materials: wood; glass
Ecological aspects: off grid electricity; sewage treatment plant

Hachi Lily House Vietnam

Architecture: SILAA
Completion: 2021
Project address: Than Van Nhiep 16/18, 530000 Hue, Vietnam
Bedrooms: 2
Gross floor area: 115 m²
Size of site: 1,300 m²
Client: Tran Khanh Chung and Nguyen Khanh Van

Hachi Lily House is located in a small pomelo village near the city Hue. At this place, privacy and the atmosphere inside a garden full of pomelo flowers can be enjoyed. The building is covered by a large sloping roof that protects from the tropical climate of the site. In front of the house, a small wooden bridge leads across a water lily pond as the main access to the veranda. The interior is composed of the common area, including the kitchen, living and dining area, two bedrooms and two restrooms. The special feature of the house are the outdoor showers in the inner garden.

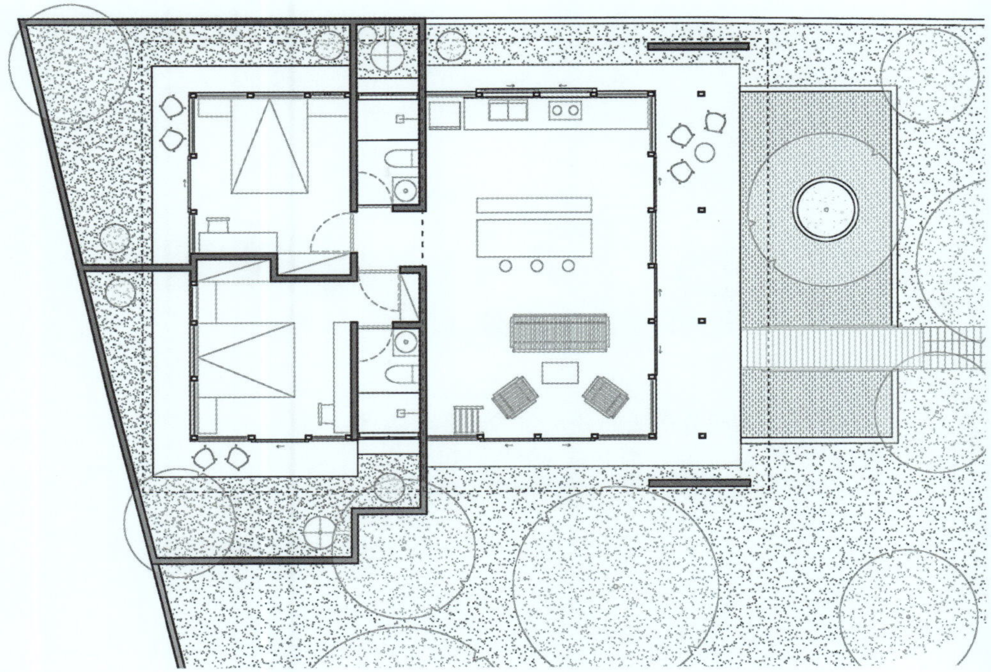

Main materials: wood
Ecological aspects: main frame, ceiling, walls, doors, windows and furniture made from reclaimed wood

Villa PJMJ Germany

Architecture: BUB architekten
Completion: 2015
Project address: Bad Kissingen, Germany
Bedrooms: 3
Gross floor area: 263 m^2
Size of site: 1,953 m^2

The single-story house is situated in a gentle hilly landscape. It is composed of a long, slender structure to the east and a short structure to the west. This creates two distinct outdoor spaces: the open space in the north-west as the entrance area and the private garden in the southwest. A straight path, accessible via steps, leads from the entrance area through the building to the garden. The path is made of exposed concrete and contrasts with the surrounding plank flooring of the living spaces. It is a connecting and at the same time structuring element between the living areas and open spaces. To the east of the walkway, children's rooms and guest rooms with bathrooms are arranged. At the rear, the private cooking, dining and living of the family is adjacent with orientation to the garden. On the other side of the path is the study with a separate entrance and behind it the parents' wing. The different heights and the cantilevered roofs acquire a lightness that is supported by the generous glazing.

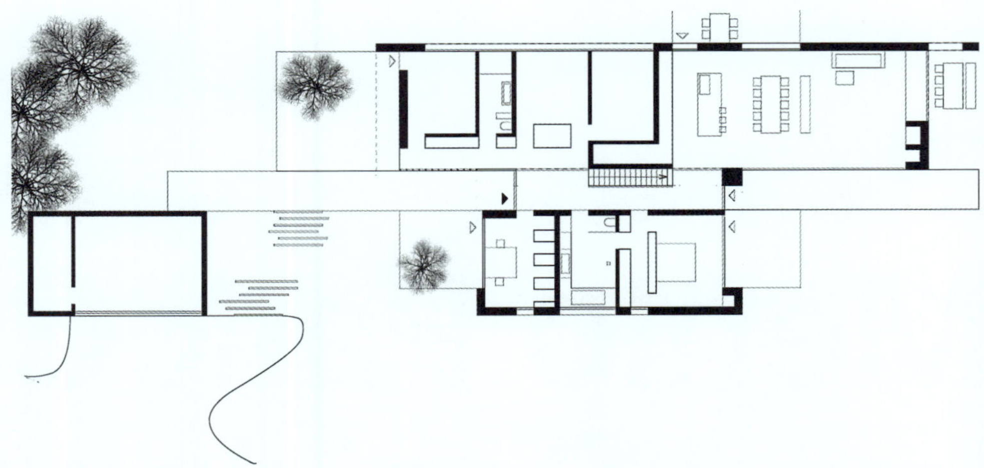

Main materials: white plaster; exposed concrete; facing stone; light oak floorboards
Ecological aspects: air heat pump

Menlo Park Courtyard Residence USA

Architecture: Dumican Mosey Architects
Completion: 2010
Project address: Menlo Park, CA, USA
Bedrooms: 5
Gross floor area: 464.5 m^2
Size of site: 2,169.5 m^2

Designed for a young family from New Zealand, the 464.5-square-meter residence located on the edge of downtown Menlo Park is a new leaf on the branch of a classic Californian Modernism. Beyond the aesthetic indebtedness of form and materials, the seamless connection to the outdoors was established as a refrain for the house's organization and articulation. The home's U-shaped plan splays apart to create an eddy of outdoor space into which drifts a swimming pool, elevated wood decks, and terraces of white sand concrete. This central courtyard flows into the great living space when a 12-meter-wide pocketing glass door opens, creating a dramatic dissolution between the indoors and outdoors. Deep overhangs shield openings from the warm Bay Area sun, and an intimate outdoor sitting area off the master bedroom is capped by a motorized awning to create a convertible space tunable to the weather and its occupants.

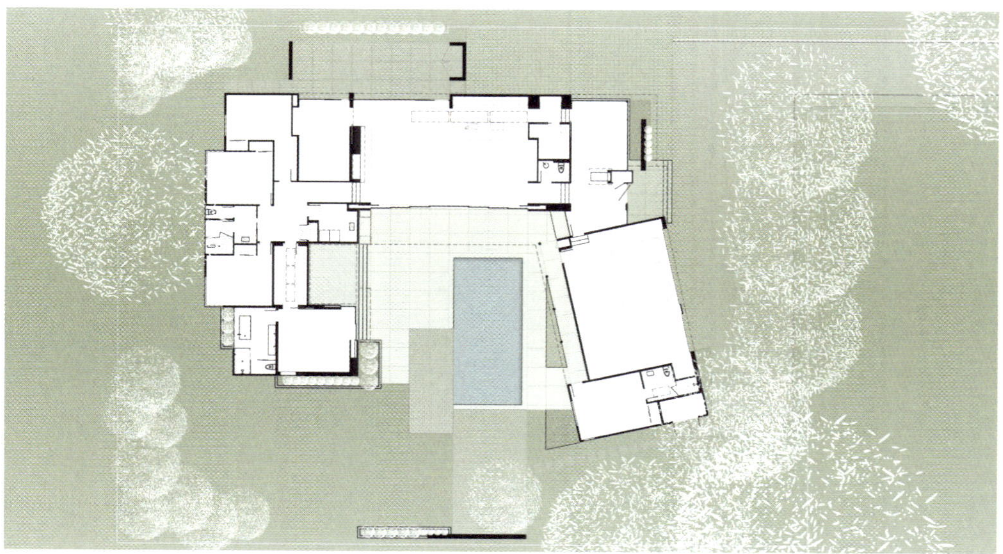

High clerestory windows passively cool the central space while acoustic plaster on the ceiling keeps the room aurally comfortable. Indoors, the structure is grounded by the same concrete floors encapsulating a hydronic radiant heating system further reinforcing the structure's energy efficiency and thermal comfort. Corrugated pre-cast concrete panels create visual anchors to organize and anchor the free-flowing interior space while providing a textural visual counterpoint to the tight lines and bright finishes throughout.

Main materials: cement plaster; tropical hardwood; concrete flooring; anodized aluminum windows
Ecological aspects: photovoltaic and battery storage system; hydronic radiant heating system; passive ventilation

Villa in the Dunes The Netherlands

Architecture: De Zwarte Hond
Completion: 2008
Project address: Hoek van Holland, The Netherlands
Bedrooms: 2
Gross floor area: 500 m^2

The Villa in the Dunes in Hoek van Holland was designed for a couple. A redesigned, sloping dune landscape is draped around the house. This creates accesses to the landscape at different levels. The main floor is on a concrete plinth containing the entrance. The concrete bunker, half buried in a dune, houses a guest house with its own front door and facilities.

The main bedroom is located on the top floor with access to a terrace. A roof staircase offers views of the sea. Two stairwells and several access points to the outside make endless routes possible. Simplicity is not a feature of this house. The pleasure lies in all the interwoven layers. The house offers a bunker, a patio house, a bungalow and a canal house. Not as a postmodern act, but in the form of archetypal transformations. This sounds pompous, yet it isn't. It's just the way this house came to be.

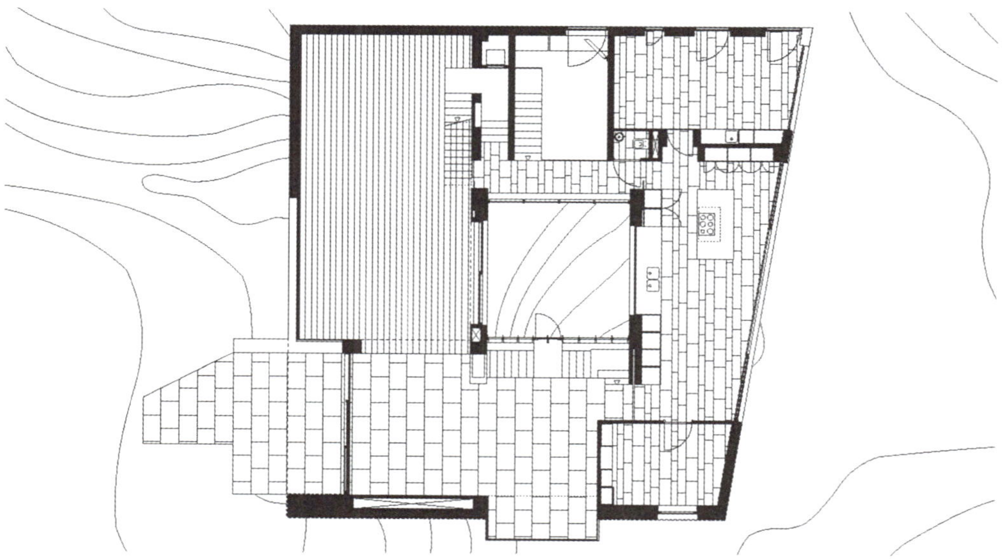

Main materials: concrete; glass; travertine and other natural stone; wood
Ecological aspects: dune garden with native local plants; neutral ground balance; rainwater discharge infiltration; heat pump

Haus FX
Germany

Architecture: Fuchs, Wacker. Architekten
Completion: 2017
Bedrooms: 5
Gross floor area: 600 m^2
Size of site: 1,562 m^2
Original architect: Kammerer und Belz
Original completion: 1969

In a careful renovation, a spacious family residence was created from two listed bungalows. The floor plan remained unchanged. It connects the entrance in the north with the park-like garden in the south and the rooms flow into each other. The light and nature from outside are brought into the living spaces via two inner courtyards and the 3.80-meter-high window walls. The fabulous view of the Rems Valley already hints at it, but only at the small gate behind the pool, where the garden merges into meadows and fields, the whole view reveals itself.

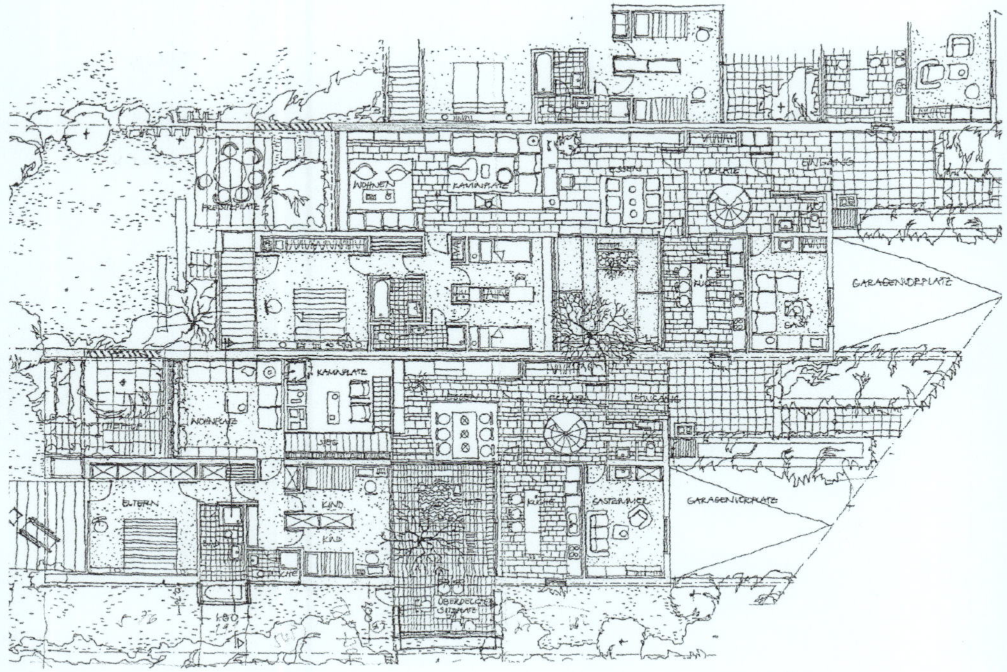

Main materials: lime sandstone; exposed masonry
Ecological aspects: monolithic construction: solid sand-lime brick not insulated; wooden roof construction insulated; triple glazing

Bungalow K Hohenems Austria

Architecture: Architektur Jürgen Hagspiel
Completion: 2015
Project address: Hohenems, Austria
Bedrooms: 1
Gross floor area: 111 m^2
Size of site: 790.8 m^2

Bungalow K Hohenems

Built gently into the hills with a wooden structure, the Bungalow K nestles perfectly into the landscape. Together with the garage, which is separated from the living area, the building forms an "L". The house was built as a wooden post and beam construction with a treated wooden screen façade. The entrance area as well as a terrace are located in small cutouts from the volume of the building. The entire living space is on one level and the layout of the rooms ensures short distances, plenty of views of the countryside and is perfectly matched for the two residents. The open kitchen-living room with many natural materials provides a cozy atmosphere. Outside, the spacious terrace with the enclosed garden offers plenty of space to relax and captivates with simple shapes. The house is located in Hohenems in Emsreuthe, at a prime location with a fantastic view of the valley.

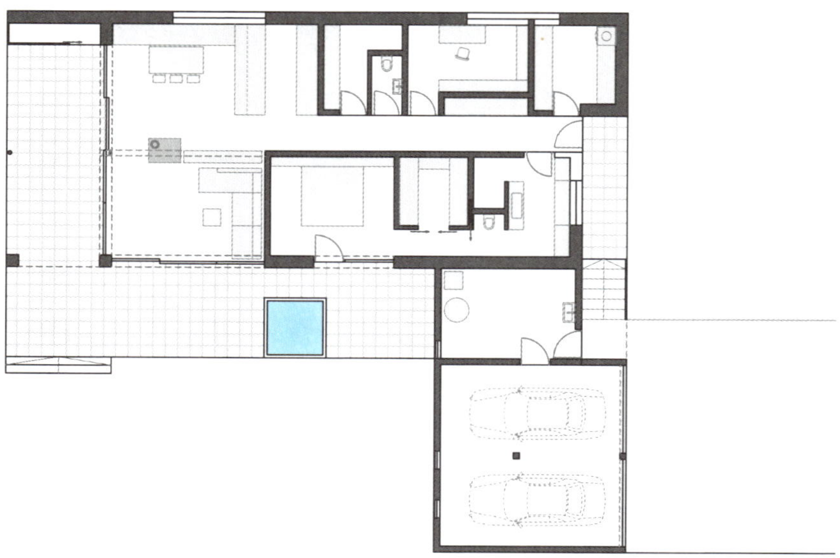

Main materials: wood
Ecological aspects: wooden construction; fireplace

Villa CD
Belgium

Architecture: OOA | Office O architects
Completion: 2016
Project address: Witte Burg Oostduinkerke, Kosijde, Belgium
Bedrooms: 3
Gross floor area: 235 m^2
Size of site: 1,014 m^2

The house is located in an allotment, surrounded by dunes, not far from the Belgian coast. Next to the strict building regulations the residents had very specific demands; they wanted to live on the same level as the street, while being protected from curious looks from passersby. The bungalow stands on the concrete plateau, which is hidden from the street behind a conical concrete wall.

The terrain slopes down by a whole level from the street to the nature behind the house. The plateau allows the surrounding terrain to remain naturally rough. The main living areas seem to float above the landscape in the back, while they are embedded in the garden in the front and connected to the street level. The plateau covers a carport located in the basement. The ramp with concrete stairs next to the slope leads to the entrance of two studios and the carport. A cutout in the horizontal surface creates two courtyards that provide the rooms with air and light.

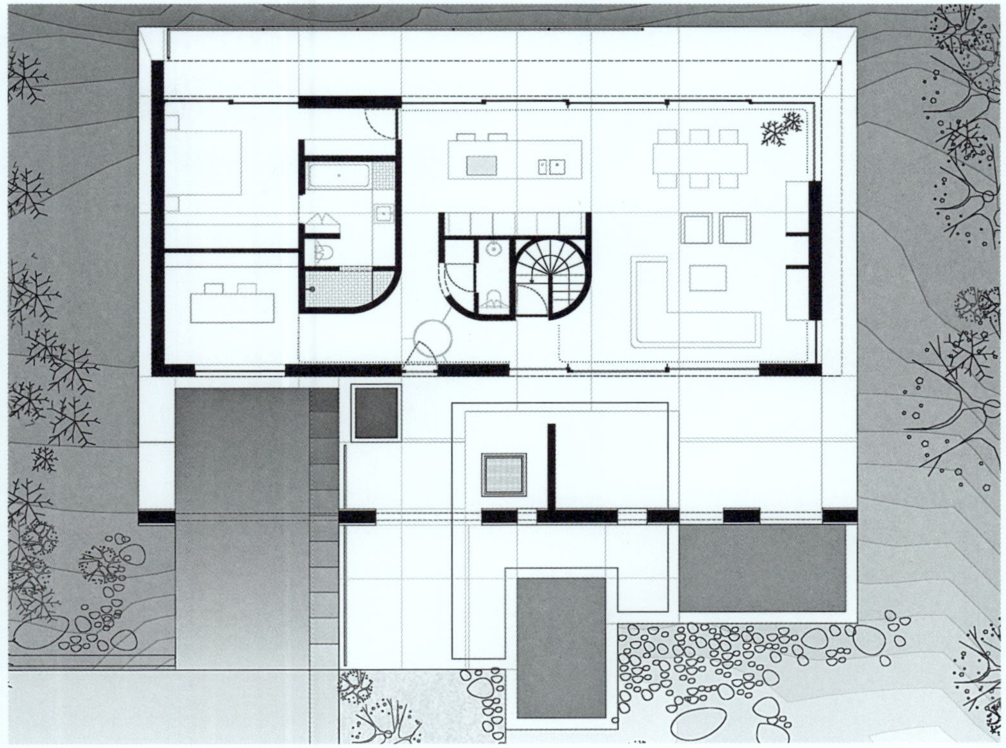

Main materials: concrete; lime sandstone
Ecological aspects: very well insulated; the house makes use of the orientation; ventilation system for extracting polluted air; reuse of rainwater

Weekend House in Nové Hamry Czech Republic

Architecture: NEW HOW architects
Completion: 2021
Project address: Nové Hamry 29,
362 21 Nové Hamry, Czech Republic
Bedrooms: 3
Gross floor area: 190 m^2
Size of site: 975 m^2
Client: David Zámečník and Petra Lehká

Based on the local nature and color, the house has an aerodynamic but angular figure where the classic elements, like the roof and the wall, merge in one. Instead of the usual two floors, three levels of action were created to resemble the character of a “lookout tower”. Inside, a special feature of the house is the second floor, which is partly formed by a net to sit in.

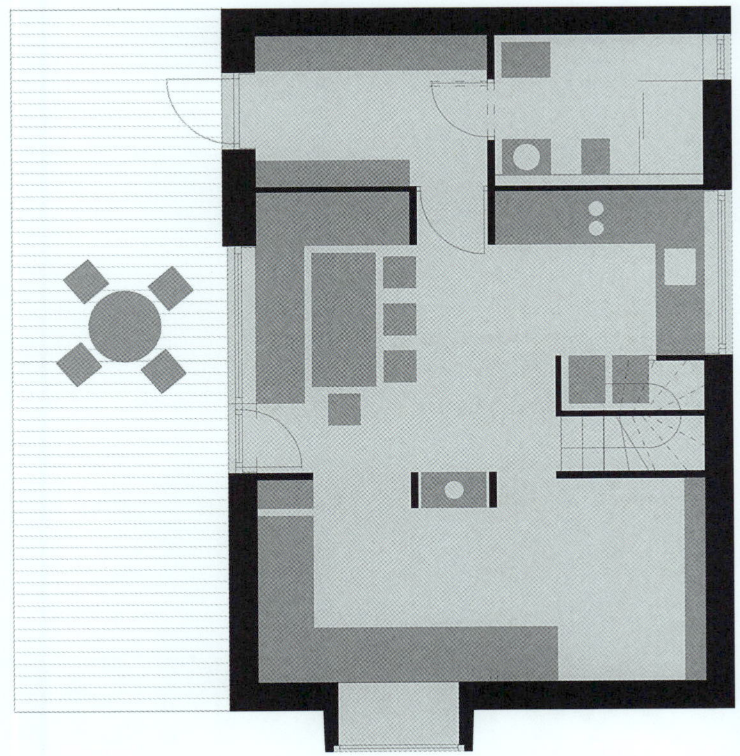

Main materials: wood; CLT panels; metal sheets; marmoleum
Ecological aspects: rational form; construction technology; preparation for photovoltaics and wind turbine to be added in the future

House in a Park Switzerland

Architecture: Think Architecture
Completion: 2018
Project address: Zurich, Switzerland
Bedrooms: 4
Gross floor area: 480 m^2
Size of site: 5,000 m^2

This park-like plot comprises a collection of single-story, freely arranged spaces. The individual structures are held together by a continuous roof edge, which creates a transition with the undulating roof landscape. The volumes take their inspiration and height from the natural contours of the area and the projections and recesses allow it to blend with the landscape of the surrounding park. All rooms have direct garden access and attractive views of the park towards the mountain panorama or towards the Lake Zurich basin.

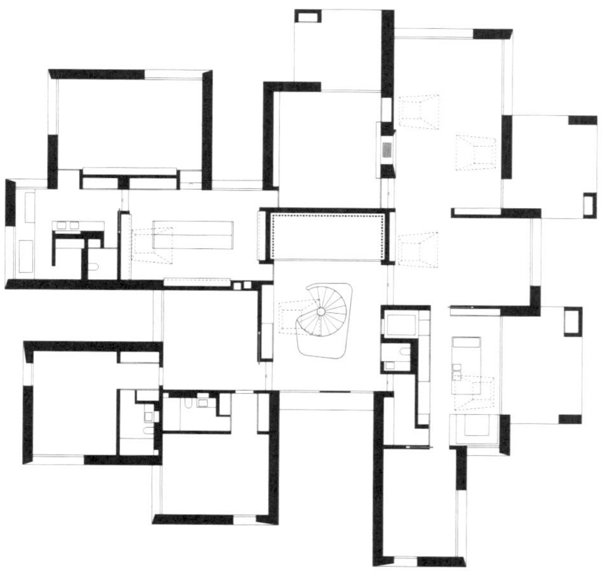

At the center of the floor plan lies an atrium that provides attractive lighting and brings living nature into the heart of the house. The underground basement is only visible near the existing supporting wall. Occasional skylights enhance the roof landscape, generating zenithal light and an additional line of sight to the surrounding treetops.

Main materials: natural stone; concrete; oak; red cedar; lime plaster; terrazzo
Ecological aspects: natural materials; careful handling of the surrounding park with the existing old trees

House Form and Culture India

Architecture: Atelier Shantanu Autade
Completion: 2018
Project address: Pohegaon, Ahemdnagar, Maharashtra, India
Bedrooms: 1
Gross floor area: 37 m^2
Size of site: 20,000 m^2
Client: Changdeo Paraji Autade

This shelter in Maharashtra is used for various activities, including storage, packaging and sale of goods grown on the farmland and providing temporary accommodation for the laborers who work in the farms. The house consists of a thin concrete wall with a prefabricated metal skeleton and a galvanized roof. In the center of the shelter is a utility and cooking area that separates the living room and the other areas. The living area acts as a multiple space that dynamically adapts to the activities and extends out to the courtyard. The courtyard also acts as a link between the rest area and the washroom.

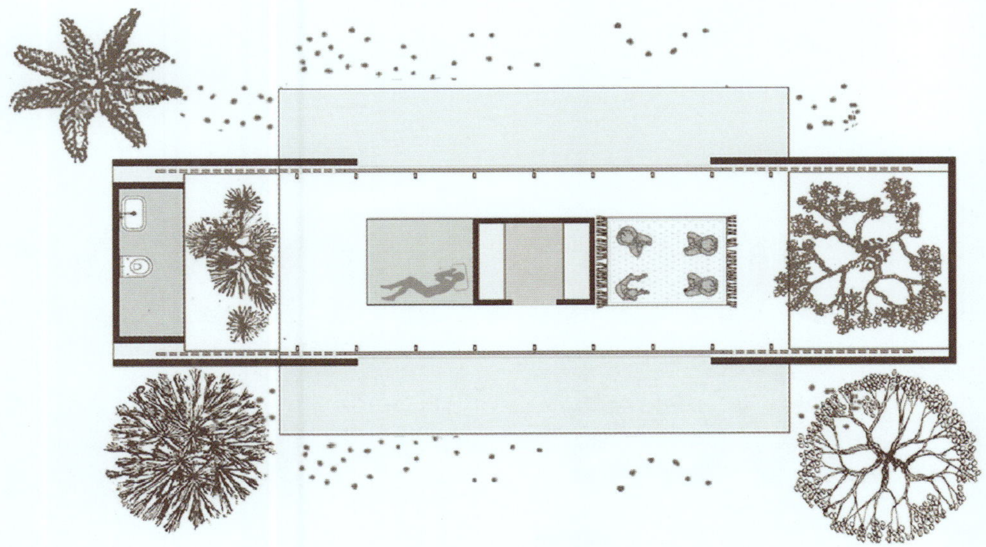

Main materials: concrete; steel
Ecological aspects: small impact on the natural environment

House Under Eaves New Zealand

Architecture: MRTN Architects
Landscape design: Bill Holden
Completion: 2018
Project address: Point Wells, New Zealand
Bedrooms: 3
Gross floor area: 240 m^2
Size of site: 1,000 m^2

House Under Eaves is located on a flat lot in a new subdivision. An oversized dark roof resting on thick cedar-clad walls protects against the elements as heavy downpours are not uncommon in the area. From the street, the front door is screened by a concrete wall that was poured in place. The house has a split gable form and the floor plan is divided into two halves: The front half houses the garage, street entrance and guest bedrooms, while the back half houses the living quarters and bedroom. A glazed connection between the two wings, that provides a second garden entrance and a sheltered space for outdoor dining is located under the highest point of the roof. The living areas are arranged on either side of a wide, cedar-clad wall that continues backward from the garden to the entrance. The high walls create space for the owner's art collection, but also give the feeling of being in a covered outdoor space, enhanced by the glazed opening to an outdoor seating area.

Main materials: cedarwood; terracotta tiles; American oak stained
Ecological aspects: rainwater is collected and used on site; PV panel array on the roof; no impermeable surfaces used in the landscape; cedar cladding sustainably harvested; LED light fixtures used throughout

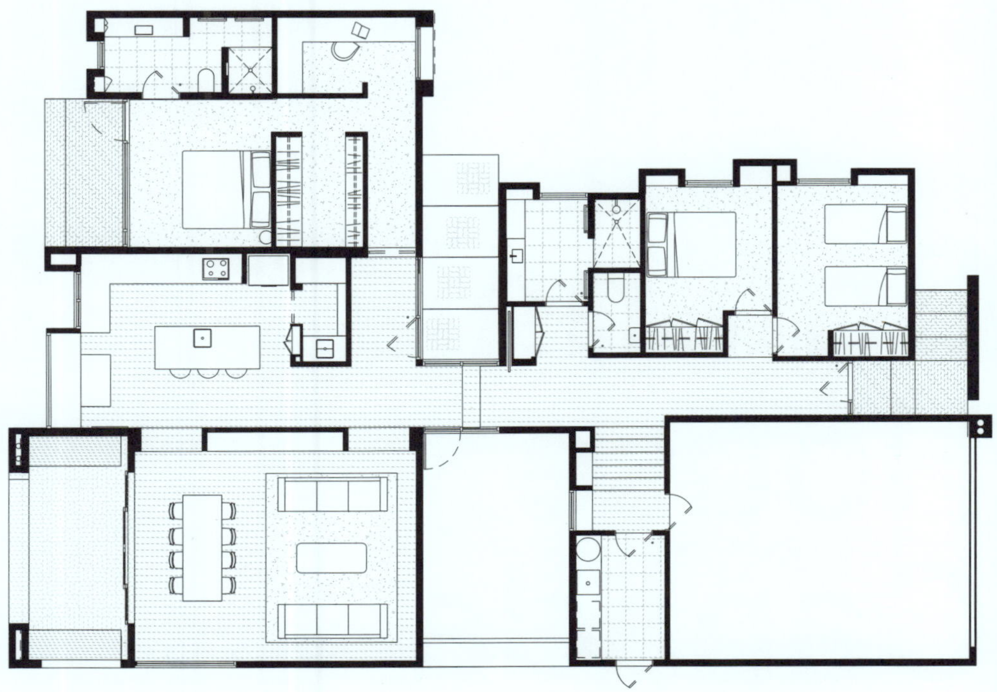

Britannia House Canada

Architecture: Shugarman Architecture + Design
Landscape design: Scatliff + Miller + Murray
Completion: 2017
Project address: Calgary, Alberta, Canada
Bedrooms: 4
Gross floor area: 395 m^2
Size of site: 1,608 m^2

4520

4520

The Britannia House sits atop the east bank of the Elbow River in south-east Calgary, Alberta. Architecturally the residence challenges current planning typologies of private and open spaces within a single-family dwelling. In many contemporary Alberta neighborhoods, the preference for family outdoor living is toward the more private backyard, as opposed to prioritizing the front porch as was done in the past. On this lot the west sun exposure and the views of the river valley below are only visible from the front yard, so the design began with an updated concept of a large covered front porch. And in order to provide more privacy, the path from the sidewalk to the front doors was carefully woven and landscaped to provide screening. The roof form in the main living space is angled up and out toward the view to take full advantage of the west facing exposure and the views of the park and river below.

The form of the house has two divergent expressions. One is the expansive space of the living area with its floor to ceiling windows and expressive roof. The other is a more architecturally subdued linear form which contains the group of smaller rooms, such as the den and bedrooms. Between these two contrasting forms lies the entry to the house, which is truly the in-between-space of the house and helps to delineate the forms and functions of these spaces as soon as one steps inside.

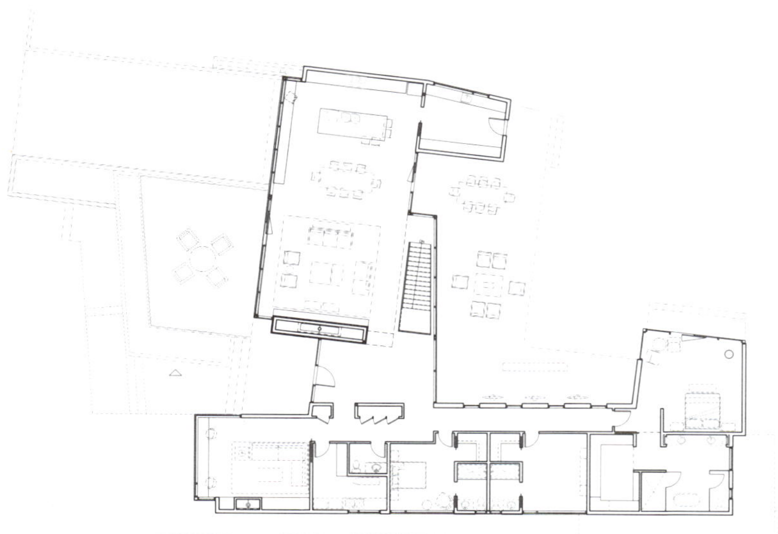

Main materials: concrete; glass; stucco; stone
Ecological aspects: sedum lawn; local plant species; interior materials produced with low or no emissions; primarily natural fibers as fabric selections; passive solar design; triple-glazed windows

Atriumhaus Germany

Architecture: Architekten Spiekermann
Completion: 2012
Project address: Münster, Germany
Bedrooms: 3
Gross floor area: 294 m^2
Size of site: 2,378 m^2

The Atriumhaus is located on a spacious site with old trees in a residential area. In the U-shaped, single-story flat-roofed house, the inside and the outside merge through the smooth transition of the floor materials and the glazing. The building appears almost closed to the outside, but this effect is reversed at the entrance, where openness comes into focus and determines the architecture. In the left wing, the master bedroom, including dressing room, sauna, integrated bathroom and a free-standing bathtub, is located. The utility room, boiler room, two children's rooms with bathrooms, and the music or office room are situated in the right wing. The open-plan kitchen, living and dining area connect both wings.

Sliding doors set into the wall allow rooms to be partitioned off, according to use. A few steps outside, crossing the atrium, you can see the living room from the outside, hovering barely half a meter above the ground.

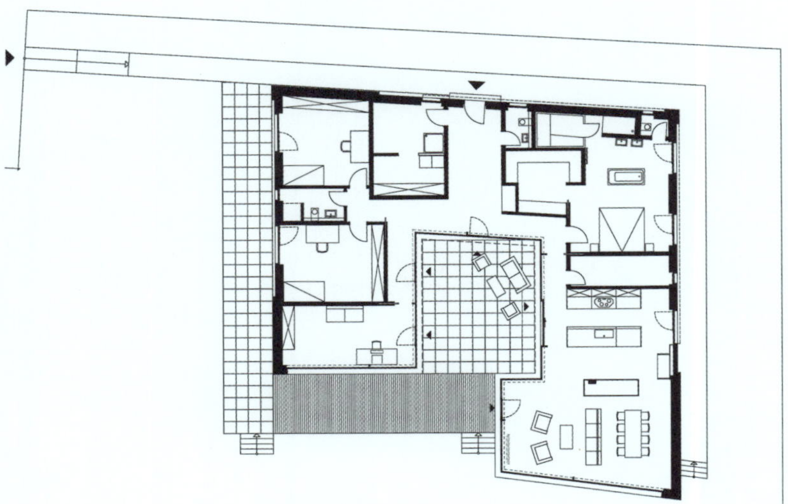

Main materials: reinforced concrete; clinker; glass
Ecological aspects: triple-glazed windows; gas condensing boiler with solar support for domestic hot water heating

Tamara Villa India

Architecture: VPA Architects
Completion: 2019
Project address: Sadar Patel Ring Road, Ahmedabad, Gujarat, India
Bedrooms: 3
Gross floor area: 650 m^2
Size of site: 6,700 m^2
Client: Sunil and Parul Patel

Located in the outskirts of Ahmedabad, the villa is inspired by tropical Balinese architecture. Every room in the house offers a view of the green surroundings or access to one of the courtyards. The house entrance, typical of Bali, leads to a courtyard with water and greenery. The landscape was designed to create a sense of seamlessness between the exterior and interior spaces. Another interesting element is the shape of the entrance waterbody. Inspired by the Udaivillas, this white marble Tamara motif becomes a welcoming part of the entrance courtyard. A lily pond with a simple graphic lawn marks the boundary to the private area of the house. The heart of the house is the living area with verandas and landscaped gardens on both sides. This part of the house has a traditional pitched roof, while the other rooms were given a floating flat roof. In the center of the house is a gathering lawn overlooking a swimming pool bordered by an infinity edge.

The interior language goes hand-in-hand with the tropical architectural language. Without using too many materials, every corner of the house looks distinct through different created floor patterns using multi-colored Kotah stone in passages and gray Kotah stone in various shapes in the rooms.

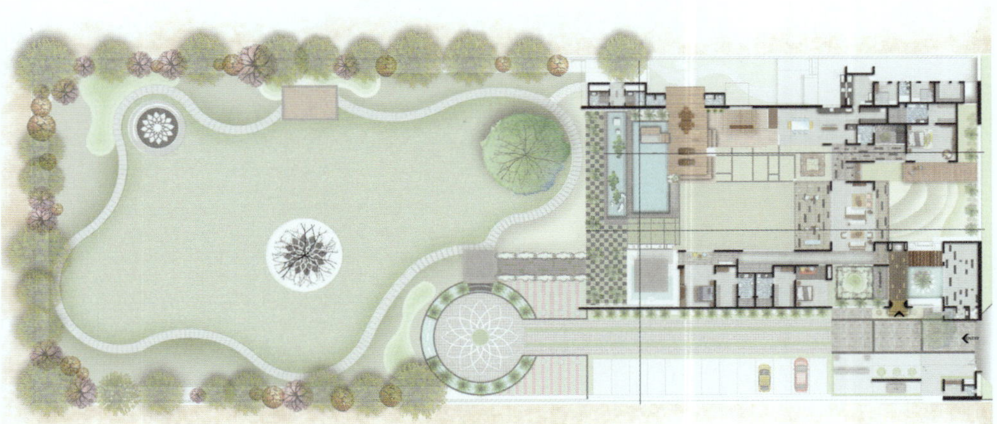

Main materials: recycled bricks; metal; concrete; glass; wood; stone; shingle roof
Ecological aspects: use of recycled brick for cladding; local stone for flooring

House L
Italy

Architecture: Plasma Studio
Completion: 2018
Project address: St. Martin, Gsies, Italy
Bedrooms: 3
Gross floor area: 157 m²
Size of site: 1,237 m²

The site is located at the edge of a commercial zone and is protected by a terrain sink from the passing-by main street in the valley of Gries-Alto Adige. As the property is sheltered by its location and has an old beautiful silver fir in the center of its generous garden, the layout focuses on highlighting the garden and forming a protection to the not much appealing surrounding constructions. The L-shaped bungalow-like structure of the project works as a counterpart to the terrain sink. At first sight, the pitched roof, requested by local planning guidelines, is not recognizable. It only becomes visible from inside the section, if seen in direct elevation or from above. Inside, the building parts used at daytime are positioned in the northern access level of the site. These ground floor living areas are preceded by generous covered terraces on the garden side. The spatial center is arranged around a fireplace, which is assigned to the kitchen and the living room.

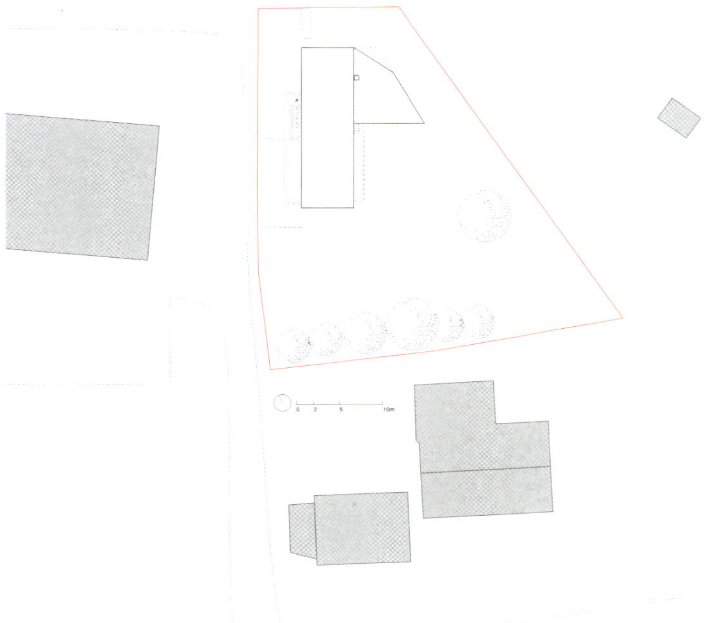

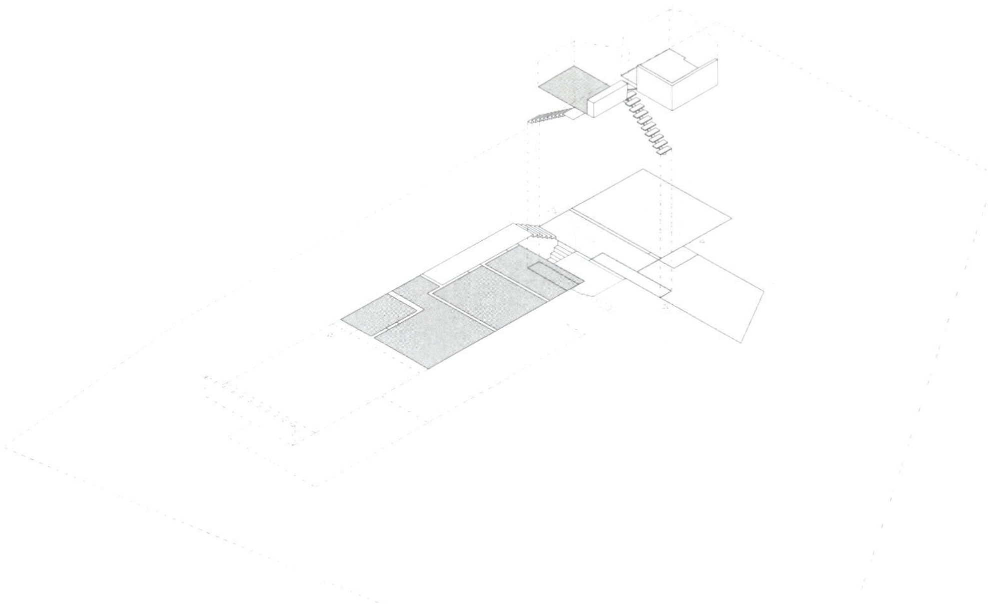

The position of the kitchen is chosen in order to be touched by the morning sun. In the living room, the afternoon and evening sun floats deep into the space. These rooms extend almost up to a double height. The bedrooms are set up in a split-level organization, have a cellar and are preceded by a simple balcony which also gives access to the garden.

Main materials: gray, vertical sawn-rough boards; galvanized and blackened steel; larch and stone pinewood
Ecological aspects: designed as Klimahaus A and equipped with a geothermal system and controlled ventilation; only local craftsmanship involved

Salt House Latvia

Architecture: Brigita Bula arhitekti
Completion: 2019
Project address: Lejas iela 21, Pavilosta, Latvia
Bedrooms: 2
Gross floor area: 245 m^2
Size of site: 1,980 m^2

Salt House is located on the edge of Pavilosta's historical center, where all the streets cross at perpendicular angles on a grid that abuts the sea. The small seaside town of fishermen, water sports fans and nature lovers has temperate climate and strong winds, so the building was constructed with thick, monolithic, lime plastered blocks without the need for additional insulation. The cross section of the one-story building was inspired by traditional fishermen's houses prevalent in the area, with an interior that opens to the building's full height and width. Within, open and closed spaces overlap, providing a semi-transparent space of both openness and intimacy. The one-story house is set in a seaside meadow as a simple, narrow, elongated horizontal volume, leaving as small an imprint in the existing biotope as possible. The architectural concept considers tradition, climate, landscape, the ecology of materials and processes, abilities of local craftsmen and many more.

The house reminds of a sand dune that catches all the salt carried by the sea breeze which gives it its name – Salt House. This idea is reflected in the natural lime plaster on the façade, which is similar in its structure and color to the coarse salt. The building will retain its elegance and beauty as it ages – cracks or leaks of rust will fit its image, because this is simply the natural order of things.

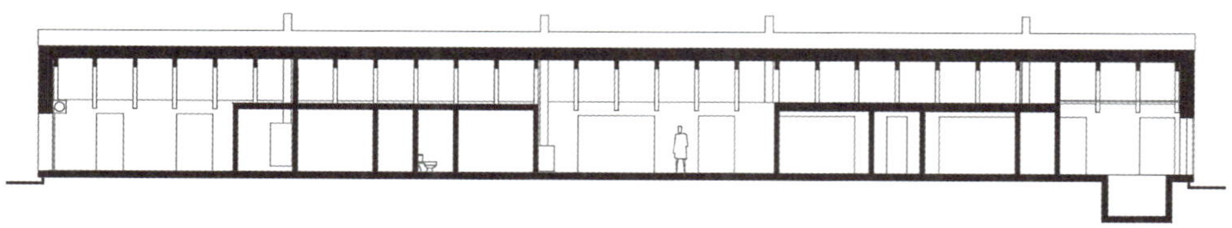

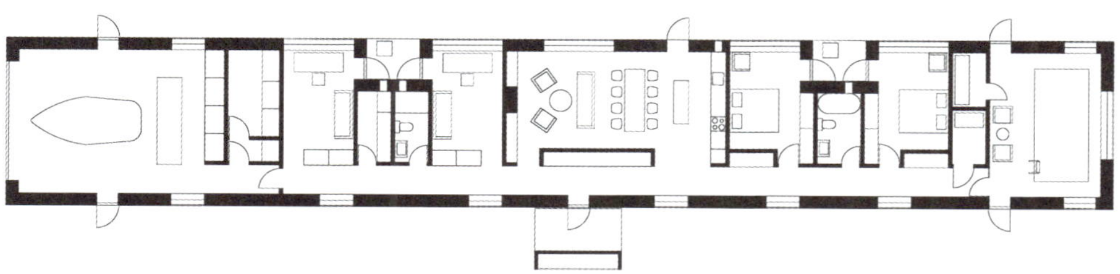

Main materials: lime plastered aerated concrete blocks; cast concrete; reclaimed wood; custom-made site-specific windows and doors
Ecological aspects: local crafts-men and builders; no additional insulation needed because of the 500 mm-thick block walls; natural materials used; recuper-ation ventilation system

Holiday Home in the Dunes The Netherlands

Architecture: De Zwarte Hond
Completion: 2020
Project address: Schiermonnikoog, The Netherlands
Bedrooms: 3
Gross floor area: 222 m^2
Size of site: 670 m^2

Manatee

Manatee

The building regulations on Schiermonnikoog are strongly aimed at preserving the quality of the existing landscape. At the same time, the island tries to distinguish itself by also being inclusive for the upper market segment. The increasing demand for luxury in terms of facilities and size is sometimes at odds with the possibilities of the building envelope. The Holiday Home in the Dunes was designed within this context. It is a modest volume with an open relationship to the environment, a lot of comfort and a high degree of privacy. Because the house is partly underground, the living area is much larger than it initially appears. The layout ensures that there are enough places to withdraw in a large group, but that the holiday home also feels cozy with just two visitors. The façade of finely sawn and dried oak wood in the open air gives the house its special character. It will only become more beautiful with weathering. The green roof completes the camouflage of the house in the landscape.

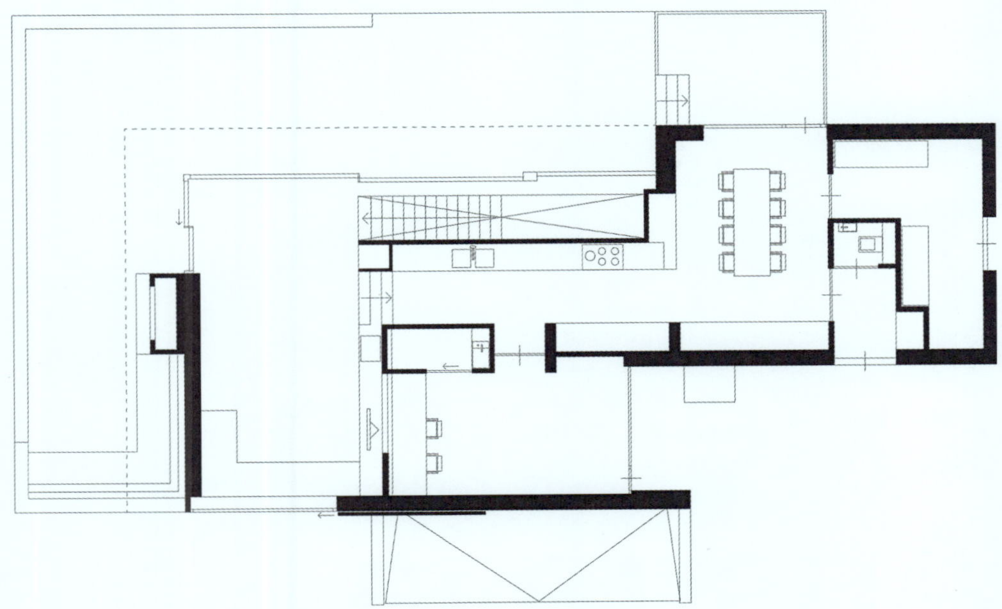

Main materials: oak wood; anodized aluminum; glass
Ecological aspects: green roofs; wooden cladding; open outdoor paving; water-saving sanitation system

Tetris Extension Australia

Architecture: Crosshatch
Completion: 2018
Project address: 83 Francis Street, Ascot Vale, Victoria, 3032 Melbourne, Australia
Bedrooms: 3
Gross floor area: 145 m^2
Size of site: 326 m^2

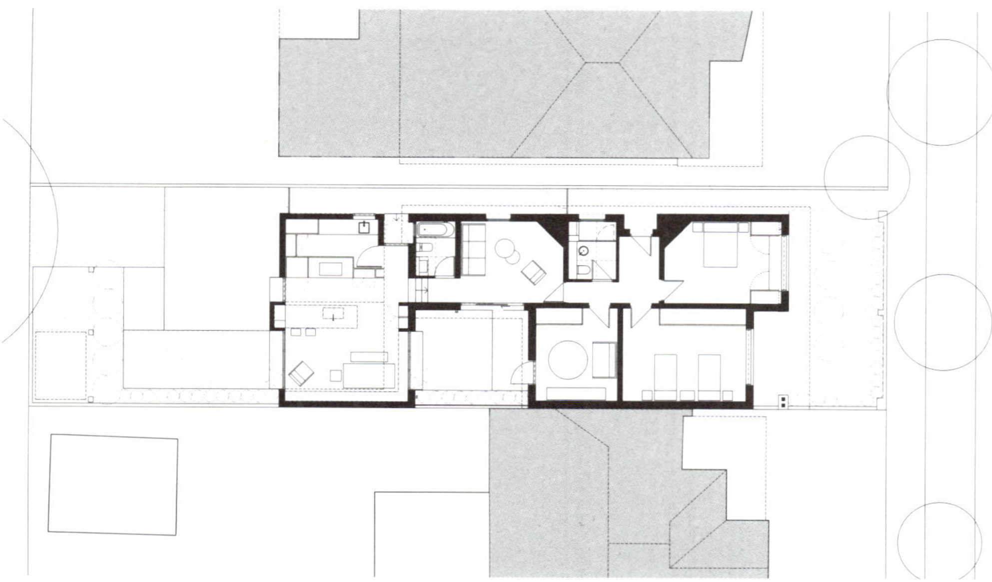

The existing floor plan of Tetris Extension was reconfigured to provide a third bedroom, additional bathroom and central lounge. The resulting extension, despite its simplicity, offers a high level of complexity and multi-functionality. Capturing northern light was a priority for the south-facing extension. This was achieved with the introduction of a central courtyard and strategically positioned windows. Bringing the outside in was an important aspect, which was realized through the dining area's large picture window with deep reveals and bi-fold glass doors that open to the central courtyard. This active green space extends the living areas beyond their boundaries, creating a sense of spaciousness. The design also allows for visual connection between spaces, so the parents always have a clear view of the children from the kitchen, wherever they are. The forms of the new extension are arranged in a tetris-like configuration, expressed in the plan, elevation and section.

The interlocking volumes unite the form and function of the old and new. The tetris concept is further iterated through the interior detailing, including bespoke cabinetry and custom kitchen door handles. Every design decision, from the smallest interior detail to the exterior's overall form, has been carefully considered to achieve a convincing approach to small footprint modern living.

Main materials: recycled red brick; steel plate; spotted gum battens; blue stone; concrete
Ecological aspects: retention of 95% of existing dwelling; passive solar design; cross ventilation; use of recycled materials

Bungalow am Schaalsee Germany

Architecture: BUB architekten
Completion: 2017
Project address: Biosphere Reserve Schaalsee, Germany
Bedrooms: 1
Gross floor area: 178 m^2
Size of site: 2,500 m^2

The bungalow at the Schaalsee creates a retreat in the biosphere reserve. The single-story bungalow appears generous and open on the small footprint. The aim was to create a simple building that offers a view of nature, but at the same time stands powerfully and confidently in the landscape with a pronounced, solid materiality. A rectangular floor plan with loft-like, large and regular openings to the east, south and west was implemented. Carefully placed facing brick in transom format divides and structures the façade through projections and recesses.

The reduced one-room concept is divided by a massive chimney block, which also acts as a holding center in the room. Room-high glass-steel partition elements create separate zones of use, but maintain the character of a flowing, open floor plan. The motive of the loft-like glass façade is also continued in the interior and sets graphically attractive accents. The incident daylight is warmly reflected in the room by the cream-colored walls. But the main actor remains nature, the old apple trees on the dewy meadow, the birds against the evening sky, the grazing cows on the horizon.

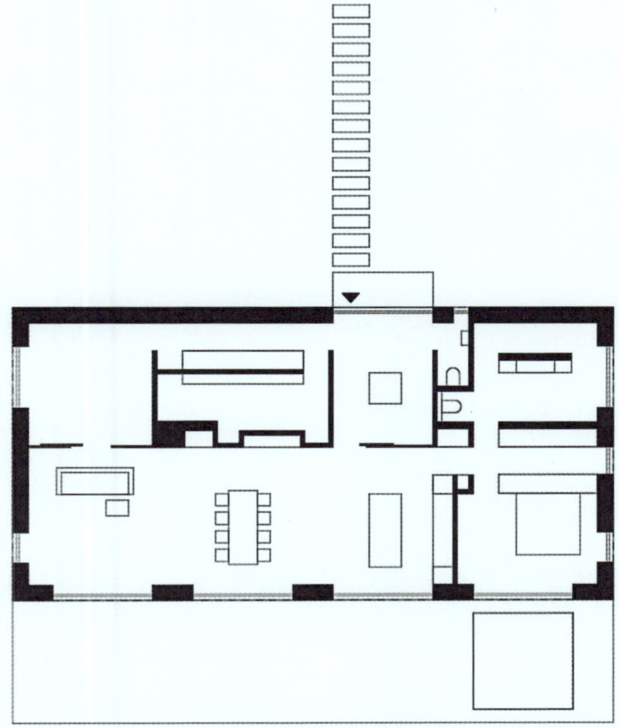

Main materials: brick; steel windows
Ecological aspects: natural and durable materials

Smokewood Garzón Uruguay

Architecture: MAPA Architects
Completion: 2019
Project address: Ruta 9, Rocha, Uruguay
Bedrooms: 3
Gross floor area: 120 m^2
Size of site: 220,000 m^2
Client: Hannah and Jaimie
Original completion: 1990

Smokewood Garzón is a rural retreat located deep in the prairies of south-eastern Uruguay. The existing ranch was transformed and expanded to adapt it to contemporary and sustainable country life, while keeping the meaningful origins alive. First, the existing wood and stone ranch, situated on the best part of the site, was renovated. Then two new wings were created at the ends to give rise to the new main rooms. This process becomes visible in their metallic exterior cladding, which creates a strong material contrast with the rusticity and wear of the old exterior.

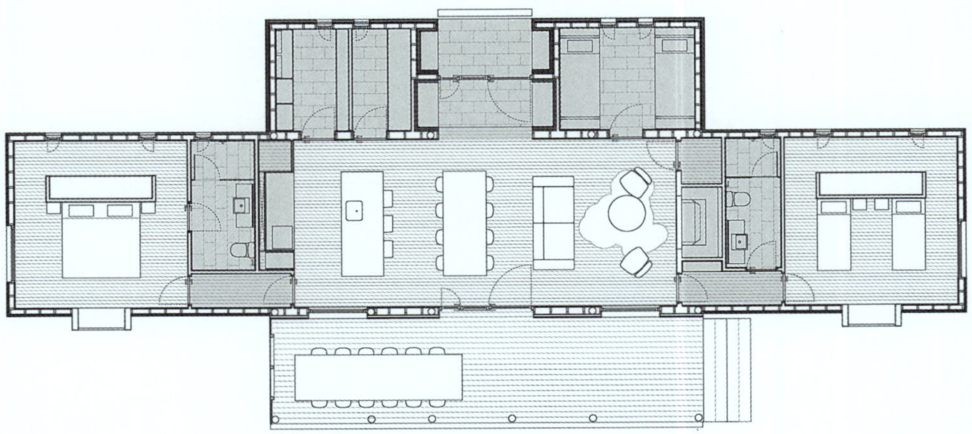

Main materials: wood; metal sheet
Ecological aspects: water and power supply systems are autonomous and self-sufficient

House S
Germany

Architecture: Architekten Spiekermann
Completion: 2012
Project address: Gütersloh, Germany
Bedrooms: 2
Gross floor area: 311 m^2
Size of site: 2,086 m^2

The walls and ceilings of House S enclose the living spaces with their straight but sweeping shape. In combination with a shell of glass, the rooms are flooded with light. It creates an atmosphere, that conveys the feeling of living in the midst of nature. The natural environment runs through the openly designed façade and inside as a floor covering of wood.

The raised floor plate causes a floating effect, which creates the feeling of lightness and the impression of withdrawing architecture that does not place itself above nature. The building looks individual due to its clear and pure forms and the colorful design. A large open living space with adjacent kitchen and dining area reflects the concept of the house and at the same time presents itself in its layout. The floor plan contains open and bright common areas for the family, but also leaves space for privacy.

Main materials: glass; reinforced concrete; white plaster; oak wood; aluminum
Ecological aspects: geothermal heat pump for hot water production; ventilation system with heat recovery; triple-glazed aluminum windows; photovoltaic system for electricity generation and storage in batteries; BUS system

Constant Springs Residence USA

Architecture: alterstudio architecture
Landscape design: BDW Landworks
Completion: 2017
Project address: Austin, TX, USA
Bedrooms: 4
Gross floor area: 335 m^2
Size of site: 487 m^2

Constant Springs Residence offers the opportunity to live in the center of the city and in an isolated retreat at the same time. The home is located in a very ordinary neighborhood, but takes maximum advantage of its location on the bluff, the creek, and the grand views behind the building. A curved roof extends over the living area, while window walls connect the interior and the exterior. The roof opens in the courtyard to enable a cedar tree to pass through, and an ipe deck allows water infiltration. A second opening in the ceiling invites light and rain deep into the center of the house. Inside, a rich palette of materials and furniture adds a sense of finesse and provides resting points for the restless and ubiquitous outdoors. In the kitchen, a Calacatta Lincoln marble countertop surrounds a vertical white oak end grain strip, while an etched mirror backsplash creates mysterious lighting.

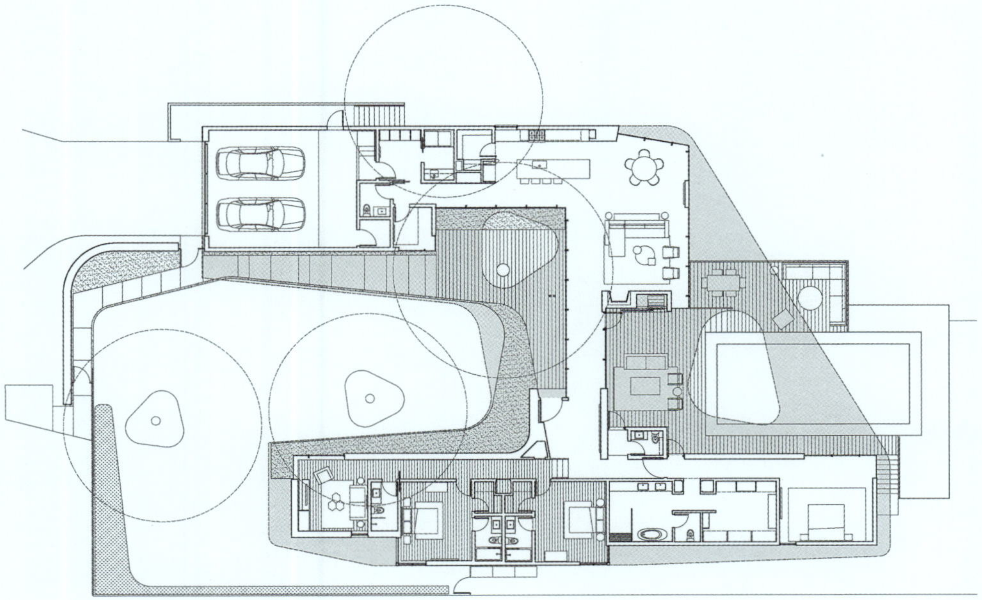

Main materials: western red cedar; white terrazzo; gray limestone; steel; white oak; glass
Ecological aspects: reduced cooling load due to shading by trees; indirect light through skylights, easy cross ventilation; optimized energy performance

Index

Picture Credits

Archmospheres
www.archmospheres.com
139–143

b-and
www.alexanderbrenner.de
137

Anthony Basheer
www.anthonybasheer.com
213–217

David Birri
www.davidbirri.com
5, 145–149

Pablo Blanco
www.pabloblanco.net
55–59, front cover b. r.

Boo Yeah
www.boo-yeah.de
129–131

Andreas Bormann
93–97, front cover b. m. r.

Simone Bossi
www.simonebossi.it
202–207

Jomar Bragança
www.jomarbraganca.com.br
4 l., 19

Zooey Braun
www.zooeybraun.de
49–53, 133–136, back cover a.

Alexandra Bub
www.bub-architekten.de
163–167, 261–265

Harry Cock
www.harrycock.nl
6 r., 249–203

Jaime Diaz-Berrio
www.jaimediazberrio.com
7 l., 255–259

Casey Dunn
www.caseydunn.net
7 r., 121–125, 279–282, 283 l., back cover b. m.

Paul Finkel
www.pistondesign.com
77–81

Leonid Furmansky
www.leonidfurmansky.com
283 r.

Rory Gardiner
www.rory-gardiner.com
99–103

Fernando Guerra
www.ultimasreportagens.com
67–71

Marcel Hagen
www.studio22.at
185–189

Reinis Hofmanis
www.reinishofmanis.lv
243–246, 247 l.

Inclined Studio
www.inclinedstudio.com
231–235

Attila Karpati
www.attilakarpati.at
89, 90 a., 91

Tali Kimelman
www.talikimelman.com
268, 269 b. l., 270

Luis Zeno Kuhn
www.luiszkuhn.de
127–128, front cover a. m. r.

The Deutsche Nationalbibliothek lists this publication in the Deutsche Nationalbibliografie; detailed bibliographic data are available on the Internet at http://dnb.dnb.de.

ISBN 978-3-03768-273-9

www.braun-publishing.ch

1st edition 2022

Editor: Editorial Office van Uffelen
Editorial staff and layout: Clara Solarek
Graphic concept: Mainstudio/Prinz + Partner
Reproduction: Bild1Druck GmbH, Berlin